A Scrappy Little Nobody

LIFE LESSONS IN FAITH, BUSINESS AND POLITICS

by
MARTIN HARDER

◆ FriesenPress

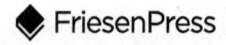

One Printers Way
Altona, MB R0G 0B0
Canada

www.friesenpress.com

Copyright © 2024 by Martin Harder
First Edition — 2024

Front cover illustration created by Raymond Derksen
Back cover illustration titled, "Joyful Journeys" created by Shirley Elias

Back cover artwork by Shirley Elias is one-of-a-kind authentic original artwork All copyright and production rights are reserved by the artist. This artwork may not be reproduced by any process whatsoever without the express written consent of the artist.

This book covers a life of over 70 years with reflections from personal experiences with family, business and politics. Challenges and gut wrenching decisions played a huge role as to who I became, and the decisions I made, and how I led. My hard work and common sense approach underscored my decisions, whether family, church, business or politics. I realised that the mistakes I made, did not destroy me, but allowed me to grow, and realise I did not possess all the answers, but needed to surround myself with great people.

All rights reserved.

No part of this publication may be reproduced in any form, or by any means, electronic or mechanical, including photocopying, recording, or any information browsing, storage, or retrieval system, without permission in writing from FriesenPress.

ISBN
978-1-03-919787-9 (Hardcover)
978-1-03-919786-2 (Paperback)
978-1-03-919788-6 (eBook)

1. BIOGRAPHY & AUTOBIOGRAPHY, PERSONAL MEMOIRS

Distributed to the trade by The Ingram Book Company

Table of Contents

Foreword: Celebrating a Life Journey of Courageous (Gutsy) Choices and Honest Reflections — vii

Dedication — ix

Acknowledgments — xi

ONE: A Glimmer of Hope — 1

TWO: Foundations of a Future — 11

THREE: Family Traditions — 19

FOUR: Roaring Fifties to Dismal Sixties — 26

FIVE: Life in the Promised Land — 32

SIX: Teenage Follies — 40

SEVEN: The Crossroads — 50

EIGHT: Teenage Marriage — 58

NINE: Adapting to Circumstances — 68

TEN: Life's Surprises — 77

ELEVEN: When Love and Marriage Meet Life's Realities — 86

TWELVE: Family Values and Lessons Learned — 93

THIRTEEN: Stepping Out into the Big League — 106

FOURTEEN: Managing Business and People — 116

FIFTEEN: Midlife Crisis and the Exodus	124
SIXTEEN: More than a Rinke-Dink	130
SEVENTEEN: A Booming Business	137
EIGHTEEN: The Deal Maker	145
NINETEEN: The Risk Taker	153
TWENTY: The Movers and Shakers	161
TWENTY-ONE: In the Mayor's Chair	170
TWENTY-TWO: The Office of Choice	177
TWENTY-THREE: The Best-laid Plans	183
TWENTY-FOUR: Life's New Experiences	190
TWENTY-FIVE: Drawing a Line	201
TWENTY-SIX: Adjustments and Opportunities	209
TWENTY-SEVEN: A Voice in the Wilderness	217
TWENTY-EIGHT: Seeing through the Clouds	224
TWENTY-NINE: Managing Crisis with Vision for the Future	235
THIRTY: A "Balanced" Approach	244
THIRTY-ONE: Reflections	257

Foreword:
Celebrating a Life Journey of Courageous (Gutsy) Choices and Honest Reflections

Within these pages lies a remarkable collection of memories—a testament to a life of courage, authenticity, unwavering faith, and farm and community development. Martin shares his inspiring story of building a farm legacy that provided for his family and supported farmers and rural communities alike.

Honest reflections are woven throughout every chapter, painting a comprehensive picture of triumphs, challenges and valuable lessons learned. Family, faith and competence drive innovation and risk taking alongside Martin's thoughtful planning and decision making.

The real-life stories transcend cultural and stereotypical boundaries, resonating with readers of diverse backgrounds and experiences and igniting a spark within each heart to live boldly. Open your mind and heart as you delve into these pages; be ready to be inspired, challenged and moved.

Congratulations to Martin Harder, a true friend and author, for this remarkable achievement. His memories remind us of the incredible power within all of us to live a brave, authentic and faith-filled life.

This book is a great read, reflecting many of Martin's farm-related memories that I previously had the privilege to write about in farming articles and publications. Many people will identify with elements of his stories, and many of Martin's earlier decisions and career moves make sense to more of us now.

May these memories guide us to embrace courage, authenticity and unwavering faith.

Harry Siemens

Harry Siemens is a farm journalist, farmers' advocate, podcaster, freelance writer and blogger, speaker and broadcaster.

Dedication

To my coach, Les Kletke, thank you for your support and encouragement throughout this process; you made writing fun.

To the great people in the City of Winkler who have given me a place to dream build and live, and given me the privilege to lead as Head of Council for 16 years of my life.

To my business partners and employees who have stood by me as a team, serving our Agricultural community with integrity.

To my readers, who have picked up this book, may it not be a book about my accomplishments, but about a very dynamic journey filled with failures and successes preparing for everything that life throws at us.

Acknowledgments

Eleanor, my first wife: for forty-six years, you had much patience with me and helped shape me into a better father, husband and leader.

Valerie, my second wife: you gave me new energy and confidence to tackle and discover another chapter of life. Your joy for life inspires me.

My family, who were patient and understanding in the process of changes in my life.

My editors, Elizabeth Falk and Debbie Maertins, for their understanding and expertise in developing this memoir into a more interesting and captivating read. My artists, Shirley Elias for capturing my life story painting as "Joyful Journeys". To Raymond Derksen for capturing the "faces of Winkler" on the front cover.

Others who helped review the material and gave feedback, especially Harry Siemens, a long-time friend, and Pastor Randy Smart for his wisdom and input.

Those who challenged me to become a more dedicated and committed believer in God, others and self.

Today I am grateful for the sustaining and healing power of God, as evidenced in these chapters; without Him and the support of family and friends, my life would have been pretty boring!

I am forever grateful - Martin Harder

ONE:
A Glimmer of Hope

It was a sweltering hot day in the beginning of August 1949, and my dad was taking full advantage of the fact that my mother was a lover of the outdoors; she was a great help on the farm. Mom's daily duties included helping Dad with outside chores as well as working in her huge garden designed to provide a year's worth of groceries. As the kitchen was not one of my mom's favourite places to spend her time, it was fortunate that her oldest girls were well trained and capable of doing the housework inside. Dad and his boys could easily have looked after the outside duties; however, I never knew my mom not to be knee deep in muck when it came to helping Dad. That was where she shone.

Summer holidays meant all the children were home, taking part in all the duties of the fall harvest season. Home was a mixed farm near Lowe Farm. Horses were still the primary source of farm power— though we transitioned later to tractor power—therefore, the challenge to complete all the tasks required many hands.

This day started out no differently than any other day, with harvest underway and stooking sheaves of grain a part of the process. My mom, whose pregnancy was now full term and at the due date, took her place on the binder where the bundles were formed and then gathered in the catch-all till just enough were formed to create a stook. Stooking involved standing up the stacks to dry the grain before it was harvested with a threshing machine. This job was generally left for the kids as a "ParticipACTION" challenge! There was no need for a gym or any other exercise program.

Dad was driving the tractor on the morning of August 6th while my mom brought up the rear, operating the binder. (In today's prenatal procedures that might have been called her "birthing ball.") My brother Peter recalls that day vividly. Mom stepped down from her duties on the binder, and she and Dad went directly to the car and drove to the nearest hospital in Morris, about ten miles away down Highway 23.

At this time, conversations would have taken place in the home about looking after the expected newborn and how the family would need to pitch in where needed. After all, I did have five older sisters and four older brothers to help with the extra work involved. As was the custom of the day, younger family members were oblivious to the fact that another child was to be born. The older ones were better informed. (Sex education was not something that was discussed around the family table but reserved for quiet conversations suitable for adults only!) All the younger family members knew was that Mom was going away, the older kids were in charge of the duties around the farm and everyone had better share the load.

Since most of Mom's other babies were born at home, having this one in the hospital wouldn't seem like a challenge. Mom had already been through eleven births; she understood the process and the risks. This was expected to be a routine trip: Mom would be gone for a week, she would come back home and life would return to normal. And yet, there was always an element of the unknown.

Well, the delivery went smoothly and she gave birth to a bouncing nine-pound baby boy! Everyone joined in the excitement of the good news. Deciding on this boy's name took a bit of time, and in the end, the name chosen for the new arrival was Martin.

Dad came home and farming continued. The girls looked after the meals and the garden while the boys helped Dad. Unexpectedly, within just a few days of baby arriving home, it became clear that something was drastically wrong with the newborn. Baby Martin would not quit screaming, and there were no dirty diapers. Many days were spent in the hospital struggling to find relief for the new baby, with no solutions to be found. As was the norm, desperate pleas were made for God to save this baby. Those cries were being heard, but even so, his condition deteriorated rapidly day by day. Mom and Dad had lost their firstborn son at birth. Their second son had passed away at the age of seven from lockjaw (tetanus), the result of stepping on a rusty nail. No doubt they experienced flashbacks of the multiplied pain of losing their first two sons. This one was number twelve, one of ten children still alive.

By the time I was two weeks old, hope for a healthy child was dwindling and my parents were desperate to find help for their starving infant—now weighing only five pounds. Receiving medical help in Winnipeg seemed out of the question. However, they heard of a certain Dr. Cornelius W. Wiebe in Winkler, who was willing to give this boy another look, a chance for survival. Out of sheer desperation, and against all odds of success, my parents took me to Dr. Wiebe for an examination and assessment. This was a time before free health care was available in Manitoba, and my parents had no money for medical services. Dr. Wiebe would have been aware of this. He admitted that he was not familiar with my condition. However, because there was no hope at all if he didn't perform an exploratory surgery, never before done on a two-week-old baby, my parents agreed to the procedure.

On the operating table, when it was impossible for the doctor to locate an artery, my arm was cut open to find a blood vessel so they could insert an IV. After I received some fluids, the doctor decided to perform the same procedure on my bowel from my rib cage to my belly button, looking to find how this kid was put together on the inside. (My brother called it "butcher surgery.") What the doctor found was an obstructed main bowel that would not allow any food to be processed or absorbed into the bloodstream. The challenge now became how to get nutrition into this frail, virtually lifeless body. By this time, my mom was no longer producing milk, and cow's milk was too risky to give to an infant. What was the alternative? By mid-August, another lady had given birth at Bethel Hospital in Winkler, where my surgery was performed. My mom remembered her as Mrs. Elias. She had enough milk for her own child and more, and was willing to feed me as well. Success was in the making! I was retaining food, I had dirty diapers and the situation now looked hopeful.

While I was being cared for in the hospital, back at home, my sisters prayed so hard that this baby would live. They wanted their baby brother at home! My sister Kathy made a deal with my mom and with God: if Mom could bring me home, she would miss school one day a week to do all my laundry. Well, as God would have it, I did come home, Kathy stayed home too and the family of ten was now complete. I believe that this incident helped shape my sister's character, creating a very caring and compassionate person.

I've experienced truth in the saying that it takes a village to raise a child. I've often wondered why I was the recipient of so much grace from God that He would allow me to live. As I recall these stories, I realize how important it was for Dr. Wiebe to be available, a risk taker working against all odds, trying something new. He was determined to explore all options, and as a family doctor, he had already earned the reputation of being the "best in the valley." I've often wondered how many guardian angels were around me then. Why was Mrs. Elias available in the hospital having a baby at that specific time, willing to help me recover? Why was Winkler the place I was given a second chance at life? How was it that, in the darkest time of my life, light still shone through others for my benefit?

Has this taught me some lessons? Yes, and yes! I believe it shaped me into a person with a solution-based mind. I developed into a risk taker and a community-minded individual. I discovered that the darkness around us is disbanded by the tiniest light and that our deepest despair dissipates with the smallest encouragement. The love of others motivates me to try and try again; the love of God is the answer to all my fears of what the future may bring. I have learned to trust and not only survive, but thrive in every circumstance that life throws my way. I have become familiar with life's challenges and have not lost hope. I have had opportunities to cultivate a loving servant heart, being thankful for friendships and for the smallest of gifts. How little I really control in my life! Everything I have accomplished is only because of God's grace, the abundance of His love and the love of family and friends!

When I take my eyes off myself and focus on others who are in need, there remains a bright future. From my earliest beginnings, God started preparing me for what He had in mind, a lifetime of discovering His ways and His purpose for me.

A Scrappy Little Nobody

Martin at three months old

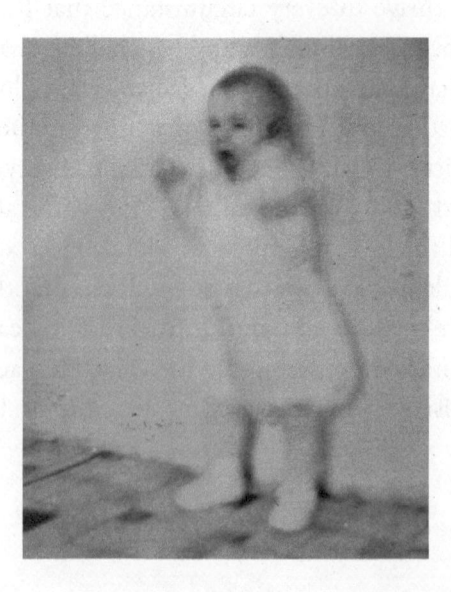

Martin standing against the wall at five months old

A Glimmer of Hope

Martin at two years old

Martin picking flowers at two years old, already into mischief

A Scrappy Little Nobody

Martin holding a huge potato at two years old

Martin at fourteen months old, showing "political leadership skills"

Mother Anna Harder looking after the outside chores in the late 1930s

Father George Harder plowing with a 4 horse team in the 1940s

George Harder custom threshing in the late 1940s and early 1950s

TWO:
Foundations of a Future

After a tumultuous hospital stay, being the new kid on the farm had its privileges. The attention I received from family, relatives and neighbours was over the top! The Harder's miracle child had arrived home at last, with all hands-on deck to take care of this new addition. However, my introduction to Lowe Farm would be short lived; later that fall of 1949, my family was uprooted and moved to the Steinbach area. (This same venture had been attempted five years earlier, the family settling for just nine months around the Giroux area, where my older brother Menno was born. That new beginning came to a premature end when my mom and dad moved back to Lowe Farm, where my sister Verna and I were born.) This time around they settled in the district around Friedensfeld, where the closest school was Oswald School in the rural municipality (RM) of La Broquerie.

My physical development "post op" was fast and furious, and I never missed a beat! No more complications. My appetite was unhindered and I grew like a weed! I was walking and talking before I was a year old. No one could ever tell how near I had come to being another infant death statistic.

Life was great. I adapted quickly to my new surroundings as a healthy, growing boy with an inquisitive mind and an action-packed personality. This created a lot of work for my parents, and especially for my sisters! My sister Kathy, having committed herself to God and my mom to take care of me, fulfilled her promise to the tee. All the while a special bond grew between us.

Our days on the farm were ordered. Monday and Tuesday were laundry days. Wednesday to Thursday were gardening days. Friday was shopping and baking day. Saturday, well, that was inside cleanup and bath day! Sunday was the day of rest where only basic chores were done. The morning was spent in church, and the afternoon and evening, either at home with guests or going visiting.

Gardening was my mom's pride, joy and passion. She continued putting her green thumb to good use, developing a huge garden that was sufficient to supply our family's needs. The question then became how can you get all your work done in the garden when there's a very mobile little one-year-old? And how can you prevent the little one from destroying the plants or wandering off to new and exciting adventures where he might not be safe?

While being outside with my mother as she worked in the garden, my exploratory mind took me to places I was not allowed to go. It was a lot of work to keep track of me, so an ingenious invention was created to solve this problem. As in most yards, there was a long clothesline strung out across the grass. I was fitted with an upper body harness attached to a leash that was fastened to this clothesline with a ring, allowing me to roam to a fixed point and not get in my mom's way. I guess you might say that this is where I first learned about getting to the "end of the line" or "the end of my rope," so to speak. Problem solved. I was able to wander, and my mom could get her gardening done in peace. I needed to have limits set for me. At the same time, my mischievous habits were being honed, and I had a lot of willing teachers in my older siblings.

I recall one moment where my mouth got the best of me. I was only three or four years old when the Watkins and Raleigh home delivery salesmen came by our farm with some regularity. I had observed that my mom preferred the Watkins products, or perhaps it was the salesman! One afternoon, the Raleigh salesman arrived, and as was the custom, my mom and dad sat around the kitchen table where the salesman displayed his wares. On this occasion, I was allowed to sit at the table to observe; I believe the rest of the family was in school.

I was fascinated by all the articles on the table and by the sales pitch. I gazed intently at the presentation, making the salesman a bit uncomfortable. He was getting a little annoyed.

"What are you gawking at?" he asked me bluntly.

My reply was swift and without hesitation. "At a monkey."

My parents' jaws dropped! As I discovered after he left, I had said the wrong thing, and I was given instructions on how *not* to speak to strangers! This was one of those sayings I'd been taught by my brothers, so really ... it was not my fault! I was a quick learner, and some of the skills I learned from my brothers may not have been the ones I should have practised.

The farm provided many adventures for a young boy. We had geese, ducks, chickens, pigs, calves, cows and horses. My mom placed high value on hatching her own birds, even if it meant placing a goose egg or a duck egg under a mother hen to hatch these oddballs. Very imaginative! Eventually a home hatchery was constructed out of a modified cardboard box, heated by a light bulb to get the desired temperature. We hatched many batches of baby chicks and ducks in this unit. Some of them experienced too many heat variations, resulting in overheated eggs and, on occasion, egg explosions. Those resulted in a horrible stench.

Some of Mom's successes produced pretty birds as well; bantam chickens were smaller but feisty. One day, I was playing in the farmyard when I saw the gander goose get annoyed at the bantam rooster. The goose had the rooster on the run, backing him into a corner until he was ready to meet his demise. It was "Custer's last stand." At least, that's how the gander saw things, until the tide turned. The rooster engaged his vertical lift, flew at the gander and got him right on the head, teaching the gander a lesson he would never forget. I never saw another conflict between those two.

It's wise to never overestimate size on the outside without considering the dimensions inside. This lesson has stayed with me into adulthood. Just because someone doesn't measure up on the surface, it does not mean they will lose the battle. A door of opportunity closing doesn't mean there's no window open to escape or that power to overcome is not hidden within.

Reflecting back to the very beginning of my life, I see that I was backed into a corner, facing the end with no way out—and still people did not give up on me. Throughout my life, there have been many times where I faced similar circumstances requiring that I dig deeper, refuse to give up and take one more run at it. I wonder how God must feel sometimes. He has provided everything His children need to complete their task, but they don't always use the energy and skills hidden inside their being.

* * *

Oswald School, 1954, would be my introduction to kindergarten. My dad was on the local board of trustees. I'm not sure if he had any influence in starting the program, but perhaps he helped speed up the process of getting me out of his and Mom's hair! Kindergarten began after Easter break, so I spent part of April, May and June in class. School was different then. There was just one room and one teacher for all the classes. The grade 7 and 8 students were responsible to assist and help teach the younger grades while at the same time focusing on their own studies. It still seems like a good system, almost like post-secondary "co-op" education, where the older students are taught responsibility by teaching the younger students.

Our teacher, Mr. "String Bean" Rempel, standing a full six feet six inches tall, was a force to be reckoned with. His size alone was enough to make me cringe! The added incentive of seeing the twelve-inch leather strap in the top left-hand drawer of his desk made us want to behave. I don't recall ever receiving corporal punishment except for one slap on the palm of my hand—I can't remember why, but reflecting on my pre-school behaviour, I'm sure I deserved it. I witnessed other misbehaving students get the strap, including my brother Harry. To this day, he still insists he was innocent and didn't deserve the strap! Accused of expecting exceptional treatment because our dad was a school trustee, he had argued that was not the case.

Harry was not quite as innocent as he claimed the day he got into a fight with the neighbour's kid, Gerry Schmidtke, on the way home from school. We lived a bit over a mile from school, so boys had a lot of time to get into trouble. My mom and dad had bought all of us new lunch kits. Mine was a smaller square metal box; my older siblings got the fancy version with a lid that looked like a hip-roof barn. Inside the lid, a wire separating the top from the bottom held the thermos in place. During his fight with the neighbour kid, my brother decided to pull out the full arsenal available to him and whacked Gerry over the head with his lunchbox, making a huge dent in the fancy new box. No easy disappearing act was possible since the evidence came home with him. Harry had to give an explanation as to how this happened, and our parents spoke to the teacher.

A Scrappy Little Nobody

Generally, in those days, adults supported each other. The two boys were separated so they wouldn't get into this kind of situation again. Nope, "Little Johnny" was not innocent, and he would have to carry a buckled lunch kit as a reminder for the rest of his school days!

Grade 1, days shared with four others in my class, was a very carefree time. Although the interschool sports events were pretty good, the school wrap-up with a picnic in June was the most memorable. It was a time to be outside and play, not necessarily organized sports, but special races including three-legged races, high jumping and broad jumping. I remember the prizes: hot dogs and ice cream in a Dixie cup as a bonus, prize ribbons and perhaps a few nickels as a winning award. Best of all was having five cents to spend as frivolously as I wished! Yep, that was huge. It was a rare privilege. There were no "allowances" given to any of us on any regular basis. I believe this taught us the value of money. Money had to be earned by hard work, and we could not take it for granted.

On one of those beautiful, lazy-daisy summer days, as my schoolmate Gladys and I were walking home from school, we decided a shortcut through the woods would be exciting—and it was! However, taking a shorter route didn't mean we got home before the rest, and we were tardy in our arrival. In my younger years, I was often teased about this childhood crush, and I didn't deny it. I had received an autograph book as a one-year-old, and over time many family members and acquaintances signed it. In the late fifties, my cousin Jacob Unrau wrote: "Dear Martin, apples are round, boxes are square, Martin and Gladys Holmes make a good pair." So, this story stuck around for some time.

Trips to school continued to be an adventure, especially in the winter. When inclement weather set in, my dad would drive us to school with the horse and caboose. This was an enclosed wooden sleigh with a stove in the back and no fire extinguisher, and a window in the front with a small slit in the centre to accommodate the horses' reins. A tanned horse hide was available in case the frigid weather got too harsh. It was almost like a modern-day RV! I always enjoyed those rides, the occasional singing that sprang up spontaneously and the odd rip the horses provided for ambience or aroma.

Cats, on the other hand … I have always had a dislike of cats! I was part of the milking crew from the age of six or seven, and one particular farm experience seriously contributed to my animosity toward cats. One day, I was sitting next to the cow and milking while the cats sat in the alley behind the cows waiting for milk. I had developed a bit of a game with them. I would turn a teat toward the cats and yell out, "High showers!" "Low showers!" and "Thunderstorms!"—which meant a direct hit at a cat's face. Well, this game carried on, but when the cow got wind of it, she didn't like it. (Likely, I also pinched her teat.) While my pail was firmly secured between my legs, at the burst of a thunderstorm she gave me a hoof and sent me flying forward into her feeding crib. The milk spilled and the game was over. I was left saddled with a dose of humiliation, plus an increased dislike of cats. After all, it was the cats' fault, no? The cats continued to annoy me. I would set down the filled pails in the alley behind the cows, only to have them place their paws on the edge of the pail and lick the foam. Eventually that was not enough and they did a deep dive into the milk. Though the edges of the pail were dirty, the milk was salvaged and separated, and the cream was sold. That may explain why the cream sometimes got sour as a result of bacterial contamination.

As I consider the lessons learned in early childhood, I can see that every experience influenced my character and my life. The privilege of having a house full of family members contributed

A Scrappy Little Nobody

to my desire for fellowship and family. That has become the cornerstone of my existence. Being a child who was allowed to explore and create my own adventures helped me to become authentic, to be who I really am, not who others think I should be. I was not enrolled in extracurricular activities to keep me busy; instead, I was kept busy doing chores and playing with simple toys. Attending a one-room school with multiple grades left its mark, and learning has become my lifelong endeavour. A teacher is not limited to one person. I was influenced by multiple people with whom I have connected throughout life, and God willing, that will continue over my lifetime.

THREE:
Family Traditions

Being the last in our clan, I was at a distinct advantage: I was able to observe how family traditions evolve and in time are challenged. For example, there was a long-standing, inherited policy that adult children leaving for work outside the home were obligated to give part of their earnings back to the parents to help support the rest of the family. As you can imagine, some family members were more willing than others to comply, and on occasion, there were heated discussions with those who disagreed with the policy. A shift in thinking would be difficult for a parent who believes the old adage "The more things change, the more they stay the same." Generally, these talks ended up with either submission to the rule or a stalemate—somewhat like the teacher in a classroom demanding that a student sit down and the child complying under protest. "I may be sitting on the outside, but I am still standing on the inside!"

As it happened, no sooner had our family resettled in the Steinbach area than my oldest sisters and an older brother were poised and ready to fly the coop—leaving seven kids around the table and a new farmstead to be developed. As was expected, my sisters were obedient and complied with tradition, giving earnings to our parents, but my brother Daniel (who called himself Donald) was less willing. After all, he was a man now, with other ambitions; farming with Dad was not on his bucket list.

Don had adventures abroad on his mind. Looking for the "opportunity of a lifetime," his search took him to a federal government contractor working up in the Arctic on the Distant Early Warning Line, or the DEW Line, as it was called. Threats of attack from the Soviet Union were very real; a target crossed the Northern tundra right into the heart of Canada, making an early warning defence system imperative. Well, my brother Don's "exit stage left" came after he applied for and got the ultimate job with good pay. Preparing to leave home, he had a conversation with my dad about the compulsory monetary contribution. This talk did not turn out anything like the one Dad had had with his obedient daughters. Don thought he would be far enough away and out of contact, and so could do his own thing. There were not many places to spend his money up North, and Don was not a foolish person, just determined to challenge the norm, which he did!

As his career choice became very profitable and his bank account reflected a growing income, my parents realized their older son was actually not that bad; in fact, he had a very generous heart. It was 1953 and our family had just received hydroelectric power on the farm—we were one of the first to get connected. When my brother Don arrived home to visit, he bought the family their first-ever freezer for a whopping $500! Even with his lucrative salary, that would have been a few months' earnings. This Zenith twenty-cubic-foot-wide wall chest freezer would store meat and the fresh garden produce harvested from my mom's huge garden. Everyone including my mom and dad were delighted. I believe that, after this happened, they changed their opinion of my brother.

Family Traditions

For those of us left on the farm, life continued to be exciting. We started with a simple routine where all the kids, myself included, learned to milk a cow by hand and then gradually expanded our work. The farm started from humble beginnings where milk and cream were hung down into the well to keep them cool. I recall several occasions when the cream can was hanging in the well, and the lid came loose, spilling cream into our only source of drinking water. Cream did have the ability to settle and so we resumed using the water, no harm done. We shipped cream, delivering it to town one can at a time; other times it was picked up at the farm. Due to the primitive storage facilities in the early years, the cream cheque would be considerably discounted because of the times the cream went sour.

Eventually, my dad increased his dairy herd and introduced artificial insemination to improve breeding. I recall Mom and Dad sitting around the table looking at pictures of different bulls with varying genetic traits, studying the history of their female offspring's milk production before they chose the semen to impregnate individual cows. It was almost like getting the Eaton's Christmas Wish List catalogue for cows! This was an advanced process, and it improved our herd to where it generated peak milk production. By now, we had progressed to a fully modern stainless-steel milk cooler. And modern "stanchions" secured the cattle in a brand-new red and black barn!

My dad was an entrepreneur, determined that every square foot of this barn would be used. When the loft was not full of bales or cut hay, it was used to raise broiler chickens. I estimate we had about five hundred up there. It was the boys' job to look after them by dragging up the water and the feed. One Sunday afternoon, while my mom and dad had company, my brother and I decided it was time to see if chickens can fly! (Perhaps that is why, in my older years, I watched the movie *Chicken Run* more times than was good for me.) On our trial run, my brother Menno, being the instigator, proceeded to pick up a chicken and heave it down to the cement pad at the barn door. Well, the first one took a while to get his breath back, so he tossed a second one. When neither of the birds got up, we knew we had a problem. First, flying was not a skill we could teach chickens. Second, now how were we going to get rid of the evidence against us? Menno decided a burial would be important. So that's what we did, only to have Dad unearth the poorly covered fresh mound, and we had to 'fess up.

My brother Menno and I were always at each other. (I am sure in his mind I was a brat.) On the other hand, my brother Peter was my protector. One day, Peter came into the barn and heard me screaming—I have to confess I likely made it sound worse than it really was—and of course, that meant my brother Menno was at fault. Since Peter was the older brother, he would take care of the situation. Menno ran for safety to the front of the cattle manger only to be caught there in a dead end. (Being the youngest had its perks!)

Trips to Winnipeg were rare, but when they happened, we were sure to enjoy the fruits of my mom and dad's trip. Normally they visited the Jewish Market, the Nutty Club and Christie's Biscuits. That meant they would come home with an assortment of nuts, stuck-together broken cookies, and kitchen wares only available at the Jewish Market. It was a grand event! Other times they travelled into the city in a half-ton truck loaded with wheat to be ground at the mill. It was not an unfamiliar sight to see ten or twelve bags of freshly ground flour, our year's supply, come home with my parents. Unfortunately, summer's heat would get the best of the bin when flour beetles made it their "home." The last few bags generally had to be double sifted to separate the bugs from the flour.

Over time, I've learned that buying items in large volume rather than purchasing them as needed doesn't necessarily save money. In fact, a product gone to waste may cost more than the money saved.

Pig slaughtering was an after-harvest, late fall event. Generally, my parents were joined by family and friends at each other's homes, where butchering pigs became somewhat of a social event, ending with a shared feast of freshly made sausage and crackles. During the day, the women, including my mom, cleaned the intestines to use for sausage casings. Yummy! The ears and feet were scraped and then preserved in whey until these parts were "ripe" to eat. Hams were salted in every crevice, smoked and stored for winter in a grain bin where they wouldn't freeze. With enough fresh lard added for most of the next year's supply, Mom would make lye soap out of the old lard.

As a young child, I was not allowed to feast my eyes on the "kill" as that might damage my mind. One day, my sister Verna and I decided to sneak into our outhouse—which had plenty of knot holes to peek through—and watch the whole event. Well, that was an eye opener for us, and nobody knew we had done that! We did survive and we still eat meat, so I guess we were not permanently damaged.

Being an entrepreneur, my dad operated a beet hoeing crew as a side venture. He would hire family and strangers alike to go to neighbouring beet growers' fields and hand hoe every row. Given he was using child labour, I am sure the extra money came in quite handy. While my job was just to tag along, I recall crawling along the rows to pick the small weeds left behind.

So, life was busy and it seemed great to me. My two older sisters got married, and Mom and Dad celebrated their twenty-fifth wedding anniversary, which made them seem ancient in my mind. At this time, they had ten kids (plus a previously deceased infant and seven-year-old, and several miscarriages). Financially, it appeared we had it made. In 1957, my dad came home with a brand-new blue Ford Niagara 300 four-door sedan. That was a beauty! Not to be outdone by his dad, my brother Don came home with his own new red and white Ford Rideau 500 two-door hard-top! I believe this respectful rivalry continued for many years.

Can you imagine the learning opportunities I had—from very modest beginnings, struggling to survive, transitioning to a modern dairy farm while family members were leaving home? Looking back to when I was a healthy nine-year-old ready for the next big event, I value having had my mom at home to give me love and attention and having my dad help me develop my mind as an entrepreneur. I am grateful to my big family for helping me grow up.

* * *

The dairy was booming and the threshing business was outstanding. Income from hoeing beets was supplementing revenue from the farm. The older kids were settled, the younger kids were healthy and Dad was a school trustee. Both Mom and Dad were fully engaged in the Chortitzer Mennonite Church. Why would that not be *the* place to settle and stay forever?

Well, yes, but now my dad's brother Bill and my mom's brother Diedrich were both moving to the land of plenty: MacGregor, Manitoba. Surely that would be so much more exciting—and no more stones. An adventure just waiting to happen! Perhaps this time, it was just a midlife crisis. My mom and dad were both forty-nine years old and, once again, uprooting and transplanting their family, willing to start over. They sold the dairy to the David Reimer family, new immigrants to Canada from Germany, in the fall of 1958—I was nine and beginning the next phase of my childhood.

Family Traditions

George & Anna Harder family in 1953
Back (L-R) Annie, Katherine, Daniel, Dora & Peter
Front (L-R) Justina, Henry,-Martin- Verna & Menno
seated - George and Anna Harder -

George and Anna Harder's twenty-fifth wedding anniversary;
four-year-old Martin in front middle

George & Anna Harder celebrate 50th Anniversary
B - (L - R) Martin Daniel Menno and Peter
M - (L - R) Dora, Justina, Annie and Henry
F - (L - R) Kathy, Anna and George Verna
at MacGregor, Manitoba in May 1981

George and Anna Harder's fiftieth anniversary; Martin in back left

25

FOUR:
Roaring Fifties to Dismal Sixties

From my point of view, life in Steinbach seemed grand. So, what prompted my parents to uproot their family, sell off a very productive and prosperous farm, and move to MacGregor?

This question has haunted me all my life. Did they want to experience a new venture, or was my dad at a turning point while moving toward the half-century mark? Did he simply need change, long to leave the stony ground we lived on and move to greener pastures? Or did his turmoil have deeper roots involving the church and religion? Since both my sisters Doris and Kathy were married and had settled down in the Steinbach area, this move would mean putting distance between our families. Why? I understood it was not financially motivated; therefore, it must have been something else.

In digging a bit further, my brother Peter helped me fill in the blanks. He confirmed that my uncles Bill and Diedrich (from both sides of my family) had already made this trek and created some of the attraction to move. (Both of these uncles were next in age to my parents in their family trees. Both had huge families; in fact, my Uncle Bill and Aunt Lena Harder ended up with seventeen kids! So, there would definitely be those family ties.) But only something stirring deep inside would have driven them to the breaking point, to what I believe was the final straw: the Chortizer Church in Steinbach was moving toward adopting musical instruments in their services, and besides that, harmony was being used by the "song leaders."

It seems this was too much for my dad. I believe my mom would not have resisted this change as she was much more versatile in her musical expressions. I often heard her sing a confident alto; she also had a very strong soprano voice and could get a song going where my dad was struggling. (I can imagine this season of testing was not a smooth ride in their marriage, but their commitment stood the test of time and survived.)

The move to MacGregor was a long ordeal. There was no call for a moving van. Rather, we tapped relatives on the shoulder to help where our family could not do it. Machinery and other smaller items were loaded up on hay racks to be hauled behind the half-ton truck. One story I recall was about a hay rack wheel that came undone; as wheel momentum goes, it passed the truck pulling the trailer down the highway!

Bigger equipment, like the tractor and the threshing machine (converted from steel wheels to rubber to accommodate the trip), was dragged by our Allis-Chalmers D14 tractor all the way through the cities of Winnipeg and Portage la Prairie to our farm in MacGregor. This was in the fall of 1958 when no bypass around cities existed. My brother Peter drove the tractor, except through the cities—my dad knew the route and drove that stretch.

This move took a number of weeks before it was complete. In the meantime, what did they do with the young kids like my sister Verna and me who would be in the way? The first two weeks or so, we lived at the home of my Uncle Bill and Aunt Lena and their seventeen kids, and went to the Path Head

School with them. Not to burden them for the whole time, we stayed with my Uncle Diedrich and Aunt Marie for a shorter period (likely one week) and shifted to the Orangeville School. In both cases, we knew that, in the end, it would not be our designated school, which would need to be in the village of MacGregor. The time in these schools was difficult, knowing we were not staying, having different curriculum and the only thing familiar being the faces of our cousins.

As the final day arrived and my parents were bringing over the last load, we were taken to the new farm. What we saw was an old, dilapidated, rickety, drafty, cold two-storey home! A promise was made: we would soon build or move a newer home to the farmstead. This was just a temporary "make do" situation. That was not much of a consolation. The first night, my brothers discovered another family was already occupying a portion of the home: a family of skunks had made themselves very comfortable under the kitchen! Their removal late in the night resulted in a horrendous stench penetrating all the old wood, and it never completely disappeared as long as we lived in that house. There was no duct work between the first floor and the second, only a hole in the floor that incidentally allowed the foul skunk odour to rise along with the warm air from the wood-fired stove that permeated into the bedrooms above.

As the depths of winter descended, it became so cold one night my brothers didn't undress as they went to bed; instead, they covered themselves with a huge wool blanket, then added an enormous black tanned horsehide to stay warm. The next morning, although a snow drift had formed on top of the horsehide mantle, the three boys, still snug under the covers in one bed, stayed warm. As for that old tanned horsehide, the last relic from a family horse—not to be outdone by a family of skunks, it just kept on giving!

Choosing a church would be another challenge. That same year, in 1958, there was a major split in the Sommerfelder Church, which led to forming a Rhinelander Church as well as a Sommerfelder Church in the Austin area. This division brought further upheaval for my parents in their search for a place of worship. Just as they had already experienced in regards to the Chortitzer Church in Steinbach, Mom and Dad would have had serious discussions about which church was better. I believe my mom won this one, with the Sommerfelder church being chosen, as it was more "advanced" (although still more conservative than the Chortitzer Church in Steinbach). My uncles and aunts chose the new Rhinelander Church where both uncles became "song leaders."

As far as I could see, this all seemed just wrong. Everything that had already been accomplished was gone, our home was dismal at best, friends were left behind, and now we were transitioning into a new community, a new church and a new school that required a bus ride! None of the conveniences we enjoyed in the Steinbach area were ours; instead, we were in a very "prairie settler" environment. You could say our lives were churning, and as a nine-year-old, I felt like I had been abandoned in a jungle of change. I needed to fend for myself or get left behind.

Attending school in MacGregor required us to be in separate classrooms, as each of the eight individual grades had their own room. For me, this was overwhelming. The only saving grace was that I could look for my sister at recess. There were no teacher assistants, and the teacher I had in Grade 4 did not seem to care that I was even there! The students were primarily Anglo-Saxons who made fun of the new kids on the block. I was constantly teased and bullied, both in class and on the playground. It didn't help that we did chores before school. I don't recall showering (we didn't have such a luxury). When it was time to clean up, bath water would be heated on the kitchen stove in the boiler bucket and the water used for bathing multiple family members—there was no waste. My boots weren't likely spic and span either, and I didn't have new clothes like the other kids. (I am sure that all contributed to my unpopularity in school.)

As I faced an uphill battle, the groundwork was being laid as to how my life would turn out. Would I be one that would roll over and give up, or would I buckle down and make it on my own? Which voice would I yield to, the depressive or the optimistic one?

Not all the kids were bullies, and it was a good thing that I eventually connected with some great friends. I made it through Grade 4 with a 64 percent grade average on my final exams and passed into the next grade. Hazel Boaz, my new Grade 5 teacher, was responsible for a positive adjustment in my attitude. She made it a great school year, and I passed to Grade 6 with an 82 percent average! I could almost convince myself that I was the "teacher's pet."

Riding the bus continued to be a hassle. The older kids were downright mean—these Mennonites stepping into their established territory would not find a welcome mat! There was a popular hit song by Claude King on the radio in the late fifties and early sixties called "The Comancheros Are Taking This Land." We were serenaded by this song, not as a compliment, but to intimidate us kids, reminding us we were considered outcasts.

How important it was to have family then, parents who cared deeply for me, giving me the love only a parent can give and especially the love my mother could offer.

While I was growing up, it was vital for me to understand the role of willpower in changing any negative situation and to decide not to follow bad examples or blame others for my mistakes. I chose to forgive when wronged and that became my key to experiencing peace in any situation. As I continued to grow and adjust to our circumstances in MacGregor, life became more balanced, with a mixture of fun events and tough rows to hoe.

* * *

"Finally, brethren, whatever things are true, whatever things are honest, whatever things are just, whatever things are pure, whatever things are lovely, whatever things are of good report; if there is any virtue, and if there is anything praiseworthy, meditate on these things" Philippians 4:8 (*New King James Version*).

FIVE:
Life in the Promised Land

Surviving that first winter in MacGregor was not for the faint of heart! It was brutally cold, and we still had to live with the stench of the skunk ordeal from the fall of 1958. Establishing the milking herd and the pigs kept us hopping, and all the while, we struggled to melt enough snow and ice to maintain a drinking water supply. Perhaps this was the time we got used to drinking Freshie (a powdered drink mix) as a frequent source of liquid consumption; rainwater did not have the most desirable taste!

Spring of 1959 came along with its own challenges—so much rain, the creeks overflowed. But since the soil was sandy, it dried out, and though the planting was a bit late, the crop was put in. Summer was busy, with my dad digging the basement for our new home so it could be moved on the yard before the next winter set in. Well, "new" was a bit of a stretch. It was an older two-storey home converted into a bungalow by removing the top storey and adding a cottage-style roof. There was great anticipation for the changeover, even though the new house was not quite finished by the fall.

Harvesting was late that year. It was October 7, 1959, my dad's fiftieth birthday, when we woke up to the wettest, biggest "snowfall of the century." With the crop in the field, three feet of snow put a huge damper on the expected harvest. The snow thawed a bit, enough for the stooks to freeze firmly to the ground with the next frost, making it impossible to load them onto a wagon. We were fortunate that thirty-five acres of oats had already been stooked, and these rows of frozen sheaves stood proudly in the field, ready to be gathered for the threshing machine. This created another challenge, yet also another opportunity; feed was in short supply and we had extra to sell, but how would we gather the stooks? My dad rented a Tourna dozer to cut a path between the rows of oats, and using the front-end loader of our Allis-Chalmers tractor, he loaded the sheaves and then sold them. A lot of imagination, determination and work was put to good use to salvage this crop.

Life on the new farm continued to call for advanced resources and innovation. We dug a pond to retain water for cattle and hogs, a great solution to the problem of not having a well, or so we thought. We had a warm home with a cistern in the basement and a manual pump in the kitchen, and *voilà* running water—as long as there was enough rainwater. If not, we hauled water from town to fill the cistern.

The summer of 1961 was a whole other experience. The last raindrops fell on May 6, my brother's wedding day, and there was not another significant rain till September, which meant little to no crop. Then came grasshoppers, by the millions, invading and eating what crops were left. With no crop insurance in those days, we tightened our belts and became ever more dependent on livestock and poultry. Obviously, money was scarce. No frills.

When water in the farmyard dugout dried up, we hauled water by horse and sleigh from another source a mile across the frozen fields. We placed a 150-gallon open horizontal tank on the sleigh together with two 45-gallon drums to fill with water and bring back to the yard. One day, my brothers and I were on a trip to haul another load. On occasion, they would take their "rabbit gun" and go for the odd hunt. This time, being the youngest and not much good for dipping pails of water out of a hole in the ice, I asked for the privilege of being the rabbit hunter while they filled the tanks. They were gracious, allowing me to wander off into the bush. Well, it so happened that I saw nary a rabbit, nor did I fire a shot. Coming back empty-handed to my brothers and the horses, I decided that, before we returned home, I would get rid of at least one shell in the chamber, which I did. But now I was close enough to spook the horses. They took off out of the dugout, sleigh and all, all the while dumping both barrels and the trough full of water off the sled. One of my brothers grabbed the horses' reins and got dragged through the snow, eventually stopping the team and bringing the horses back to the scene of my crime, where all the containers had to be reloaded. This time, I was the one scooping most of the water from the hole in the ice. I don't recall ever being invited to come along again. I wonder why. Kid brothers are not always the greatest asset.

Not to be down and out because of the drought, but as time moved forward, it seemed to leave nothing but more disasters in its wake. On a bright, sunny Sunday afternoon in 1963, my family went to visit my cousins' place. Nothing unusual, except that this day as we came home, we saw our barn fully engulfed in flames, with some younger calves, all our pigs and our tractor still inside the barn. This was the worst nightmare for a farm family to go through. We saw pigs jumping out of the barn, running through the bush while dripping burning fat, starting smaller fires as they ran. Over the course of several weeks, a few surviving animals were recovered, but we really didn't know how many got out. A week or so after the fire, we discovered one of the bigger boars had dug himself into the bottom of the creek and was healing his wounds in the mud!

This one did survive and was nursed back to health, then fattened up at my brother's place, only to end up as sausage and crackles in the neighbours' freezer.

Starting over once again, we had to rebuild the barn and replace the livestock. My dad was a good carpenter. He had renovated the house he bought; put up the basement, one cinderblock on top of another; and installed a cistern sealed with tar to keep it waterproof. My mom was by his side every step of the way, making cement mortar, getting her hands into the tar, sanding and painting inside and outside walls. They had that figured out together! Now they designed a new barn; it was to be a hip-roof style similar to what we had in Steinbach. The beams on this structure would be fully laminated from the base to the peak. One rafter measured twenty-four feet to the peak. To create this framework, Dad designed a jig, placing seven layers of one-by-twos, glued and nailed together on the flat side. To complete the task, sixty-four half-rafters were constructed one layer at a time. We all participated in one way or another as time allowed between other chores that needed to be done. It was amazing to see this building come together, how the rafters all fit into place to create an extremely sturdy barn!

I have a fond childhood memory of playing in the hayloft of my Uncle Abe and Aunt Susie's barn during an auction sale. These events tended to be treated as social outings around the neighbourhood. The ladies' auxiliary generally brought pies or baked goods, the men actively bid on the goods being sold, and the kids, well, we just went off to play. On this occasion, I was fortunate to have my cousin Peter visiting me from Steinbach, so we went along to the sale with my parents. Well, there were a couple of girls that I noticed: my cousin Betty and her friend, who were playing together. We decided we would all go and play in the hayloft where there was dry cut hay or *hacksel* (as it was known in Low German). My cousin Peter grabbed a handful of the chopped hay and threw it at the girls. It landed squarely in my cousin Betty's friend's face! I am not sure why, but I felt sorry for her and went over to help her brush it off. Getting a close-up look at this girl, I discovered she was very cute. Or perhaps I noticed she was very cute and that's why I helped her. Regardless, at the age of fourteen, that was my initiation into taking notice of girls, and this girl was twelve. There was no further connection between us for a few years, but she would show up in my life again.

Meanwhile, school days continued. Time spent riding on the bus depended on the route, and we travelled on the bus for a full hour or hour and a half each way. Usually, the heckling started off with me sitting in the wrong seat, but that didn't change regardless of where I sat on the bus! I still can't understand why Mr. Stone, our driver, or Mr. Brisco, our spare driver, never came to my aid. Surely, they would have noticed something. My schoolmates' misbehaviour carried over into school. I was not an avid sports fan or great sports player. All the same, being chosen for a team was a school requirement, and a few of us were always the "leftovers." We were eventually assigned to a team, but I was always one of the last to be chosen. That was not a confidence builder, and I became a bit of a recluse, dreading another team selection process.

One day in Grade 8, I was playing soccer on a team and really wanted to make an impression. I got possession of the ball and squared myself to give that fake pigskin a huge kick. I didn't care where it went; all I knew is I finally got the ball! I aimed and hauled off a wallop, only to have the star player of the team snatch the ball from my foot and I ended up bashing him squarely on his kneecap! For this "offence," I was sent to the principal's office and given several weeks detention. My schoolmate Garnet Lee was away from school for some time, healing from his crushed kneecap. At least I didn't have to go through the rejection of being last for team selection for several weeks. But can you imagine how my popularity diminished even further by taking out a star ballplayer?

In my family, being the last kid didn't mean I got to play all the time. My responsibility was being the "trade-off guy," who would run the tractor while my brothers took a lunch or coffee break. One day, I was plowing the field over a lunch break. I left from the edge of the field, and on my first pass, I discovered a bright red package of Du Maurier cigarettes lying in a furrow about midfield. Of course, I stopped to pick it up but since "no one" in my family smoked ... how did it get there? Not to give this up easily, I went to my brothers to ask if they knew who it belonged to. (Well, I actually knew, but pretended it was a surprise to find such a new treasure in the middle of the field!) In the end, I negotiated a deal: if my brother gave me two cigarettes, I wouldn't say anything to Dad.

My next chore was checking a mile of electric fence. My brother lit the cigarette for me, and off I went! Lots of alone time to smoke it and air out before getting back. Since I did not want to be caught with any evidence, I bravely decided to light the second cigarette off the lit butt end of the first. Big mistake. I got sicker than a dog, lying on the ground actually crying out to God to save my life and promising never to smoke again! God came through that day and I didn't die. I wish I would have been as dependable in keeping my own promises.

Going to church was a weekly event. One of the reasons we ended up going to the Sommerfelder Church was that they had a regular Sunday school class that was a bit more geared to younger kids. Once children were past the age of twelve, they tended to sit with the adult audience; that was where I became aware of my mother's musical talents and skills. I often heard her rehearse with my dad when he was preparing to lead the singing on a Sunday morning; at home, it was a struggle.

Generally, my dad got the melody right and would do fine at church. At times, however, he struggled with a new hymn they had practised. I remember it all so well. My mom being the submissive type—after all, only men were allowed to hold any leadership position in church—would quietly sit in the audience giving him time to sort this mess out. When all seemed to go sideways with no resolution in sight, she would begin the song from her place in the congregation, bellowing out the correct tune just the way the song leaders did, getting the men going in the right direction. I often chuckled, thinking, "Yes, man is the head of the house but the wife is the neck that turns the head!" No different here. Visibly, there were only male song leaders, but behind the scenes, as in our case, it was the support from Mom that made Dad look good. Eventually, we ended up with an organ in our home, and with that, harmony came out and beautiful music filled our home. Just as Mom and Dad worked closely together in the varied tasks on the farm, they combined their skills in Dad's role as a song leader.

Mom and Dad were not always in agreement in life situations, but somehow, they resolved their differences. This left our family with the distinct message "Whatever life throws at us, we don't give up; we press on and finish the job." On Sundays, we'd postpone unimportant projects and complete the important ones first before leisure time consumed our energy. Sundays were designed by God to give us a break from the burdens of the week, not to complicate life and add more industry simply to fill our day. I believe extracurricular activities were discouraged on Sundays because it was to be a day of rest. The issue then became the definition of "rest."

On Sundays, Mom and Dad often had the travelling minister who spoke in our church come to our home for lunch. They were excellent hosts, and it was pretty special, without exception, to find an extra seat at the table. Relatives would always be welcome without an invitation; they would simply either call to say they were coming over or not call at all and just show up. Sometimes there were rifts between my dad's brothers, and one or another absented himself from our home for months until reconciliation took place. Relationships were always eventually resolved, not by one brother insisting the other come to apologize, but by one or the other deciding this just wasn't right and taking the first step.

As an adolescent, I understood I was not the decision maker, although the smaller decisions I made would have a huge impact in how I handled things in the future. As I observed, I saw how people reacted to conflict and noticed how they reacted to tragedy; my character was being developed every day into who I would become. I discovered my dad was resilient. He never gave up throughout the setbacks but continued to push forward to the next project. I understood in my early teen years how my dad managed money, or didn't manage it well, and that had a huge impact on my choices and growing ability to handle financial decisions.

I learned that the negative examples I lived with did not need to impede my future; I could use them to make good decisions that would enhance my future opportunities. I became very aware of my healthy body and that I owed it to a choice my parents made for me, even before I consciously expressed a single preference in my life. Most of all, I knew there was still something missing in my life to make me complete. That is another story yet to be told.

SIX:
Teenage Follies

It was the fall of 1962 when my dad purchased a brand-new baby blue GMC half-ton. Wow. What a beauty! Periodically, I was able to drive this truck to help load bales on the farm. On one occasion, while the truck was parked close to a stack of bales, I proceeded to move the elevator closer to the truck to make it easier to load the bales. Well, the ground was not quite level—the bale elevator flipped over, right on the cab of that brand-new truck. I don't recall getting a tongue lashing, but the cab never got fixed as long as my dad owned the truck. A constant reminder of my mistake!

Working with neighbouring farmers always impressed me. When it came to the annual corn silage harvest, we worked with the Cornelius Sawatzky family. Their son, Ed, owned a Lanz one-cylinder diesel tractor, which operated the silage cutter. He had to do extensive service on this tractor, which needed greasing many times in a day. Ed was never in a hurry. It did not matter how rushed we were to move the next load; if it was greasing time, he stopped and greased the tractor. The fields always got done, the loads hauled and stacked in the yard then covered in straw or bales to seal them. From there, the silage was allowed to ferment before it was fed to the cows. This stockpile sometimes sat all winter and was used on a daily basis. When spring came, this stack was very "ripe" and sometimes had a fair amount of liquid at the base. One fine day, our pigs got out of their pen, wandered across the creek and got into this oozing mass of silage. We heard the animals screaming, and as we checked it out, we discovered they were walking on their knees, unable to stand on their front feet! Well, as hilarious as it looked, it was very obvious they had sucked up a fair amount of "liquids" from the silage and were totally drunk. No harm done and the pigs were returned to the pen to sober up.

* * *

What happened on November 22, 1963, became a vivid memory in my life, introducing me to the world political stage. I remember it so well. One of the high school boys had a transistor radio with him, and the two of us spent some class time in the washroom listening to the live broadcast of President Kennedy's assassination. Tragedy had struck. This time, it seemed that world order had come to an end and it was devastating. I remember the teacher came to look for me and abruptly returned me to class as if nothing had happened! I don't recall much of any discussion about this monumental tragedy, other than that the focus of life in our classroom needed to be brought back to the subject at hand. I recall very clearly how that historic event brought a new perspective of life into our home. We did not have access to a TV, so we followed the news on the radio to stay up to speed on the ensuing state of affairs around the murder of President Kennedy.

It was during this time that the temptation to fit in became so great that I thought it would be cool to walk around with a cigarette pack in my shirt pocket. Perhaps then I would be accepted as one of "them." I was given some money for school supplies; however, I decided to skimp on what was essential, leaving enough money to buy a pack of cigarettes. I thought menthol would be a much better choice than my previous experience. I hid them well, and one evening as I was doing chores, while attending to the milk parlour, I simply wanted to take them out of my jacket pocket for observation when my dad walked in. I was caught red-handed, even though I had no intention of lighting one up—that would be pure suicide! My dad proceeded to confiscate the goods and I continued to finish the chores.

Lucky for me, or so I thought, we had my Aunt Lena and Uncle Bill Harder drop in for the evening. The visit went remarkably well, and as was the custom at the time, good byes on the porch were a prolonged affair. That gave me just enough time to get into the house, climb into bed, turn off the lights and pretend I was sleeping, even though my guilt was killing me! Well, my dad knew better. After the visitors left, he came to my room, slowly opened the door, and informed me that I was really not sleeping and there was an outstanding issue we needed to discuss. I was ushered into the living room, sat down and informed of my choices: I could sit there and smoke in front of my dad, or I could get the quicker treatment on the behind. It didn't take me long to make that decision, I would accept the faster pain rather than the longer duration of embarrassment. After that was settled, however, my dad decided it might be better after all if I simply showed him how to smoke. As I was going through this ordeal, I clearly remembered my first encounter with smoking and the promise I had made to God. Here I was again, the same lesson not learned, still only trying to feel accepted in school. While I was reluctantly smoking, painfully embarrassed and controlling my inhaling, Dad told me, "Son, when I see people smoke, it comes out of their nose or their ears; they even smoke circles out of their mouth. Show me more." Well, lesson learned, and I have never had a desire to smoke again! My dad kept that pack displayed on his writing desk for what seemed like years, just as a reminder for me.

* * *

Turning from the age of fourteen to fifteen was likely the biggest year of change in my life. During the summer of 1964, I had occasion to meet up again with the cutie I'd met in the hayloft at the auction sale—this time it was at a ball game. Sunday afternoons, I snuck away from home to the rural school district of Path Head where my brothers and I, and the neighbours' kids, came to play baseball. This was to be a day of rest and going visiting was okay, but playing baseball was an activity that would have been frowned upon. During this period of my life, I was making decisions outside of my parents' involvement or knowledge. I had developed a bit of affection for the cute young girl, whose name was Eleanor. I loved being around her and tried to impress her with my athletic abilities playing ball. My skills improved dramatically now that I had a good reason to do well! I learned that, whatever I tackled in life, if I had incentives to do better, those motives helped me progress to a higher level.

These Sunday afternoon outings became somewhat of a regularity and left me hoping for sunny Sundays all summer long! I recall those days as being carefree and optimistic. Life on the farm had improved with the new barn. We had transitioned to a modern dairy once again, with surge milking machines and a milk parlour where we no longer separated cream. Instead, we shipped whole milk. My brothers had jobs and drove some pretty fancy cars. On occasion, they even allowed me to drive and practise up for my own driver's licence. Periodically, I was able to give Eleanor a ride in the car, but those occasions were pretty rare.

Fall meant going back to school for Grade 9, and for the first time, I entered the doors of MacGregor Collegiate. I had also started attending youth meetings at the local Evangelical Mennonite Conference (EMC) Church where my friend Eleanor attended. We were not dating, so to speak, but this experience opened my eyes to a different style of church. I was introduced to a youth choir where I enjoyed making new friends. My parents were not pleased that I didn't stick with my Sommerfelder friends, but because I was a fairly decent kid most of the time, they tolerated it.

School was interesting. I knew I was not an athlete and I needed to find other things to do. Eleanor was in a grade lower than I and, therefore, not at MacGregor Collegiate my first year. Nevertheless, I found that spending time with the girls was interesting. For some unknown reason, there were ping pong tables set up in the girls' change rooms. I was never there when these rooms were used as change rooms, but I have to admit, I spent plenty of time playing ping pong with the girls!

We had a history teacher named Mr. Williams, and I was always impressed how he could ask us to turn to a certain page, indicate the chapter and how many lines down, and continue to recite without error every word on that page. Our principal, Miss Collier, was known for the sound of her high heels scrape-clicking on the hallway floor as she made her trek to class, so we had plenty of warning before she arrived—and the guys would quit pestering me. I could not afford Brylcreem but used another gel product as gooey and stiff as you can imagine, and I meticulously groomed and slicked back my hair. The popular boys in my class saw this as their target and liked to mess it up. I was so annoyed and refused to associate with them, not that they cared. It drove me further into thinking I was of no value.

School became a very difficult place for me to be and I hated it.

* * *

The fall of 1964 came along. I was fifteen and in Grade 10. I thought this was the year I would be motivated to do well at school because my friend Eleanor was now in Grade 9 in the same school! By this time, I knew her fairly well, and we had spent many youth events and choir practices together. It was fun, but the desire to attend school was shattered once again when the house belonging to my brother Peter and Margaret burned to the ground. My dad was there to help, and I decided I needed to be there as well and left school. Though it was a year of difficulties, through it all, I maintained my friendship with Eleanor, which helped me adjust to all the upheavals.

Leaving school at fifteen with no job other than working on the farm with Dad meant being dependent on the farm; the support from my parents would continue, along with their control over what I did. I won't say I didn't need supervision or guidance as I continued testing for solid ground underneath my feet. On a number of occasions, I had dreams of returning to school, but my formal classroom days were over. I would never graduate from high school. Instead, my thoughts turned to getting a job.

I have discovered that learning is a lifelong experience, whether in the classroom or in the school of life. I have also come to realize that making good decisions is a lifelong battle, choosing between doing what's right and what is harmful. I understood the value of work, but I'm not sure I understood the value of play. Even something as basic as riding a bicycle was missing from our home; it was something I learned while vacationing in Steinbach at my cousin's place. Owning a bike didn't happen until my teen years.

Family holidays were not something I experienced. When my parents went to visit my aunts and uncles in Winnipeg or Steinbach, we stayed home to take care of chores. It was tough to achieve a balance between work life, church life and social life. I believe I became too focused on convincing myself of my own worth at the expense of other relationships that held me accountable. I needed to understand that God valued me for who I was, not for who or what others thought I should be.

Early 1960s in MacGregor; Martin at the new milking parlour

Teenage Follies

Eleanor Bornn at eleven years old

A Scrappy Little Nobody

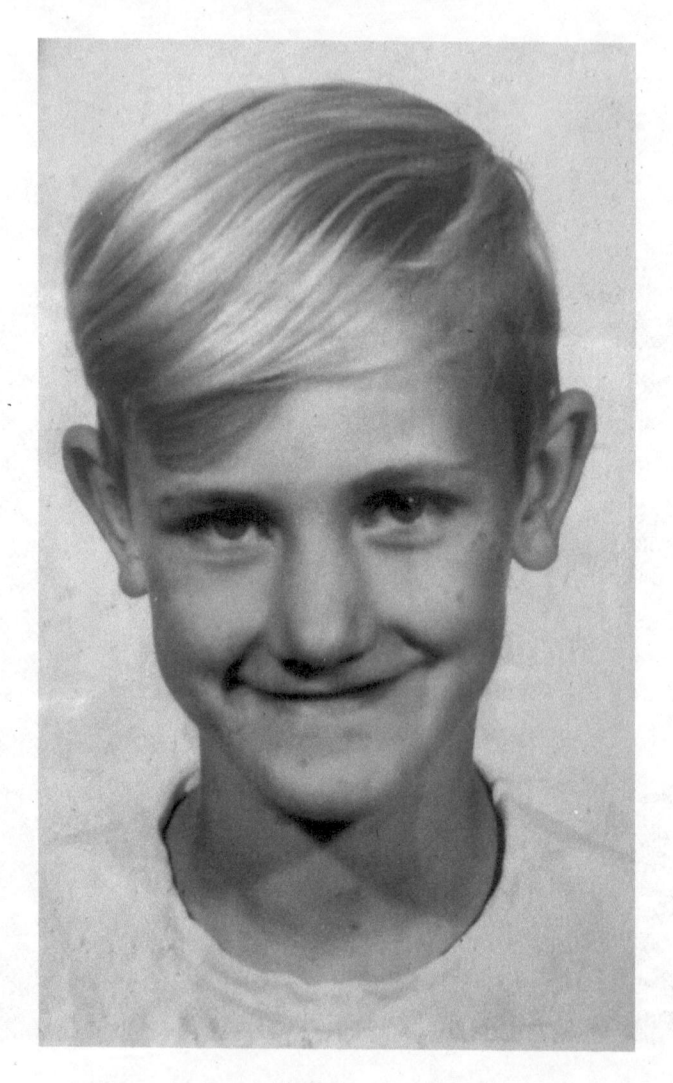

Martin at ten years old

Teenage Follies

Martin at sixteen years old

SEVEN:
The Crossroads

Never in the history of my life had the choice between two paths been more critical or more obvious than in my teen years. Being sixteen meant that any decisions I made were my responsibility, not someone else's, and I would bear the scars or reap the rewards.

My urge for adventure was pretty high, and the motivation to become self-sufficient, even greater. My dependence on my parents had diminished; however, they continued to provide guidance and advice, even though at times it appeared to me they really didn't know much.

It was in this context that I ventured out to get my driver's licence. My father agreed and took me to Lye Motors in MacGregor to verify that I was old enough to drive and to vouch for my abilities. No one there had ever seen me drive, and I don't know what qualified them to approve, but with my dad's support, I proceeded to the licensing office and was awarded the "privilege" to drive. Having an official licence meant I would have more choices when it came to various events, like deciding for myself which were appropriate to attend and which were not. I found out quickly that I didn't need a driver's licence to be exposed to wrong choices. On one occasion, as my mom and dad took a very rare week-long

The Crossroads

holiday trip out West, two of my brothers decided it was time for a "party" at the Harder household. Well, that did not end well, with liquor flowing and questionable characters at a party that lasted till the wee hours of the morning. Not a great decision for me! It was very obvious I was being pulled in a variety of directions; I would need to come to grips with who I was and who I wanted to be.

Another time, I was cruising the streets of MacGregor and Austin looking for "chicks" and seeing my guy friends with their girls. My cousin Eddy had the hots for a girl named Mary Anne, and I made a wager with him that I could pick her up if I wanted to. The bet was on, so I took a spin past her house and asked her if she wanted to come with me for a ride. Not that I really wanted to take her out, but I simply wanted to prove to my cousin that I could! She said yes. So Mary Anne and I paraded the streets, passing Eddy and his friends to prove my point. Not a wise or considerate way to treat a friend, or the girl!

Meanwhile, I decided I would look for a job and found one at Carnation Foods in Carberry. The established requirement at home remained stringent. If I went to work, I would face the dreaded rule of contributing to the family's financial resources. At first, I received a whopping allowance of five dollars per week while the rest of my cheque was deposited in my parents' account. By this time, I had settled down a bit on the girlfriend front and chose to date Eleanor on a regular basis. She helped me discover a different lifestyle and our relationship started to gel. Now the challenge was on. How could I have any outings with her on five dollars per week?

A half dozen young guys from the area were working at Carnation, so we carpooled. The driver would collect a buck a day from each passenger, so that meant a payload of four or five dollars a day. This set my entrepreneurial juices in motion!

I decided I would buy a 1959 two-door Chevy Biscayne six cylinder three-on-the-tree standard for $400. I borrowed the money based on the anticipated success of my business endeavours. Doing the math, with four passengers I would take home twenty dollars per week plus the remaining five bucks from my paycheque—which had been adjusted to ten bucks because I was providing my own transportation. With gas costing twenty-eight cents per gallon (yes, *per gallon*), the total cost of gas was only one buck per day. Plus, the payment for my loan was forty bucks per month. I thought I had it made! A girlfriend, a job, a car and friends. What more could I need?

I spent the summer of 1965 around Niverville working at the farm of my sister Doris and her husband, George. It was a good job, not far away from family yet far enough away that I was able to make decisions on my own. I had been seeing Eleanor periodically for a few years, and things were changing. I really cared for her, and she was pretty attached to me. The only other mode of communication at the time was by letter, and we wrote each other weekly, if not more often. But I was starting to see my life from her perspective: she was having second thoughts about my priorities and my heart's loyalties. Eleanor was very solid in her faith. She had a deep understanding of what that meant to her and what it would mean for the connection between the two of us as we approached the biggest crossroad of our lives. Her desire was to date someone not simply for convenience but "for real," someone who was on the same faith page as she was.

I received a note from her suggesting that perhaps our relationship should end. She backed it up with words from her Bible that said it is wrong for a believer to be "yoked" or joined with unbelievers.

The Crossroads

"Do not be unequally yoked together with unbelievers. For what fellowship has righteousness with lawlessness? And what communion has light with darkness?" (2 Corinthians 6:14).

It stopped me in my tracks.

Was I really a Christian like she was or was I just along for the ride? I asked my sister Doris, a very firm believer, what it meant to be "saved." Was it really that important? Carefully, she explained what that meant and then asked if I was ready to make that commitment.

Of course! I did not want to end my relationship with Eleanor! And yes, having learned to make my own decisions, I saw that now I could actually choose the direction my life would be heading. So, I knelt alongside my sister and made the most important decision I would ever make, one that helped steer my path going forward. I shared this exciting news with George, who advised me with the words of Romans 10:9 (NKJV): "that if you confess with your mouth the Lord Jesus and believe in your heart that God has raised Him from the dead, you will be saved."

Well, this meant I could not keep it a secret. I needed to share this great news—first with Eleanor. She was ecstatic! There would be an immeasurable transformation in all my decisions. Since George spoke regularly at Union Gospel Mission in Winnipeg, he invited me to tell my story there ... publicly! Scary as that thought was, it was another necessary move in what turned out to be a momentous change for me.

Imagine the elation of my sister Doris. Her brother had made a vow to follow God, and she had witnessed it! Satan of course was not happy, as he continued to put doubt in my mind, taunting me that I made the choice to obey God just to keep my "girl" and that was all. I struggled with this mental and spiritual debate right up until my baptism two years later. If I had made the decision to follow and obey Him in order to keep my girlfriend, then on my baptismal day, the choice would be between Him and me. Before I was baptized, I cried out to God, "I believe Jesus Christ took the punishment I deserved for offending a holy God and accepted the forgiveness and new life He offered me and I now pledge my life to you, God, so that when I share my testimony, it is not what I have done, but what YOU, my Lord, have done in me!"

I am not naïve enough to believe or suggest my temptations were over. Far from it! What made the difference was that now I understood what Jesus had done on the cross for me, a sinner who was simply saved by grace, by the shedding of His blood on Calvary. Not by works that I had done, simply by what God provided through Jesus.

"For by grace are ye saved through faith, and that not of yourselves; it is the gift of God, not of works, lest any man should boast. For we are His workmanship, created in Christ Jesus unto good works, which God hath before ordained that we should walk in them" (Ephesians 2: 8–10).

You see the crossroads I faced after the directional choices I made that summer? It was very clear this crisis would have a lifelong impact, not only on me, but on the lives of all those I would associate with later in life.

Unlike me, Eleanor was a young girl when she made that same choice, and not in any dramatic way. For her, it was a natural response to a question from a mentally challenged boy in her school, who asked, "Do you know where you will go when you die?" How profound, yet how simple! That is still the most important question we all need to ask ourselves. God used an innocent child to reach this beautiful girl, who in turn helped me understand that works would not provide me with a ticket to eternity in Heaven. I have been forever grateful for Eleanor's wise and thoughtful resolve not to allow our love to interfere in a vital decision that we both needed to make.

I am grateful that Eleanor continued to stand by my side to help me understand the Scripture and find strong Christian friends who I still cherish to this day. She helped me find a life-affirming church where I could learn more about my faith and discover ways to serve others. I faced some headwinds from my parents, who couldn't really understand why I was attending a different church and wondered what was wrong with the church where they attended. I will say, they changed over time. They understood and supported my decision, even if it was years later. They saw the evidence of the difference God made in my life, and I am grateful.

I continued dating Eleanor more seriously. It looked like I had chosen the right girl, and she thought she had chosen the right guy! Along the way, we still faced painful challenges, but we always worked them out, remembering the promise we made, even at the ages of fifteen and seventeen. I am still grateful for great friends like Bill Esau and Sharon Giesbrecht, two people with whom we regularly hung out while they supported and encouraged us as teens.

* * *

I carried on with my job at Carnation until I decided that perhaps I didn't want to work shift work all my life. I quit and found a job at Tecza Mercury in Portage la Prairie. After a month, they discerned that I was probably not cut out to be a mechanic, so I was fired! That was a new and humiliating experience, the only time in my life that ever happened. I was seventeen and thought I could conquer the world!

At the time, the Portage diversion project was underway, so I got a job filling tie rod holes with grout on either side of the beams. Not exciting, but better pay. The winter after I turned eighteen, I drew my first and only unemployment cheque. I was also working at home again on my parents' farm, saving my U.I. money to buy my sweetheart an engagement ring. It was at that time that I had a falling-out with my dad. Once he realized I was getting a cheque, he thought I should also give him part of it. Well, that was the last straw. I made it clear to him what my intentions were and that I was done supporting his endeavours.

The fact was, I was not impressed with his money management. It seemed the longer he farmed, the deeper he went into debt. If the bank would not lend him the money but Household Finance Corporation would, to him, that meant it must be a good decision. That was not my idea of managing finances, and it was an eye-opener. I resolved to never allow a bank to tell me what I should do. I would attempt to be debt free as soon as possible and make my decisions by the standards I thought appropriate.

The lessons learned in this period of my life would set the stage for dealing with new and sometimes daunting experiences in the next chapter. Saving up for Eleanor's engagement ring was a challenge, but by Easter, I had put away enough money from my unemployment cheque to make the purchase. Traditionally, at seventeen, Eleanor was still considered her father's responsibility and under his control. At the very least, it would be a gesture of respect if I asked him for Eleanor's hand before I presented her with the ring. It took a while for me to get up the nerve.

To help make a smoother meeting between us, Eleanor arrived in their home singing a song that had hit the charts in 1968 from a mother-daughter duo, Lynn and Liz Anderson: "Mother may I, may I marry? I found a love that's true." I am sure Eleanor's dad heard this singing before I ever had my heart-to-heart chat with my future father-in-law. In the end, getting parental approval was easier than I imagined. Receiving both her dad and mom's blessing was such a relief.

I gave Eleanor her engagement ring for Easter. We had already made a commitment to each other when she turned sixteen, so I knew what her answer to my proposal would be. We were so blessed to be able to clear away any obstacles for a great start in building a life together, resting on the same foundation of our faith in Jesus Christ.

EIGHT:
Teenage Marriage

The stage was set and the engagement ring, secure. What could be so hard? We were in love. We had committed our lives to each other and our future together into God's hands. With Eleanor's curfew firmly in place, we continued dating. When the evenings got a bit long, as we sat in the car in the Bornn's yard chatting (and yes, there was some kissing), Eleanor's dad, Peter, would go to the yard light switch inside the house and turn it on and off a few times. Time was up! One more kiss and Eleanor would go into the house.

After her father gave his permission and both parents had given us their blessing, we were officially engaged. Now the rumours went wild! There must be a teenage pregnancy and we "had" to get married! A marriage between a seventeen- and eighteen-year-old? That would never last. The challenge was on to prove the rumour mill and the predictions wrong.

Wedding plans began in earnest. Many decisions would need to be made. Where and when would the ceremony take place? Also, we were not baptized, and now it became important in our Christian walk that we take that step. Not that we had resisted it before, but in those days, it was expected that before you got married you would be baptized and join a church. Added to that, it was thoroughly ingrained in my mind how important it was to honour my parents according to the fifth commandment in Exodus 20:12 (NKJV): "Honor your father and your mother, that your days may be long upon the land which the Lord your God is giving you." What to do? Would we stick with the EMC church we attended in our youth or would we align with my parents in the Sommerfelder Church? So, there we were caught between two churches. Would I let down my father and mother and permanently leave the Sommerfelder? If not, then how could I think about disappointing Eleanor by asking her to join the church of my parents? In retrospect, I can see that I was lacking in maturity, because my family's pressure won.

To Eleanor's credit, she agreed to join the Sommerfelder Church, with an understanding that after we were married, we would revisit this arrangement and decide together where we would land. In the meantime, as a consequence of my choice, our wedding plans were a bit more conservative than they would otherwise have been. It was understood that Pastor Abe Neufeld from the Sommerfelder Church would officiate at our wedding, and the song leaders would choose the "Wedding March." We were allowed one attendant each, so Eleanor's friend Betty Unrau and Betty's boyfriend (also my friend), Jake Kehler, were our bridesmaid and best man. And though the wedding itself would take place in the Sommerfelder Church, the reception would be in the MacGregor Community Hall. This way, we could satisfy both ends of the spectrum; a bit of a compromise, but for now it worked.

It was August 4, 1968. A little sprinkle of rain that morning slightly flattened the delicate yellow and white Kleenex carnations taped to my newer 1962 black and red four-door hardtop Chevy Impala, but a bit of moisture did nothing to dampen our spirits at the wedding. Eleanor had been granted permission to wear a white dress ... but to exchange wedding rings and kiss my bride? Well, that happened after the ceremony was over and outside the building!

After the wedding ceremony, the ladies' group from the Sommerfelder Church catered a delicious dinner at the community hall, which was soon filled with the laughter of family and friends and music by our EMC youth group. Eleanor and I were married and on our own! That night, our friends Bill and Sharon followed us to our home located close to Helston in the bush. They helped us unload our wedding gifts. Eleanor and I spent our first night at the rented place where I intended to farm. Our home was furnished with a total of $600 worth of furniture. Eleanor had given up her job as a nurse's aide to marry me, and she was on unemployment insurance. I had a few bucks in my pocket and a credit card I borrowed from my brother Menno (for incidentals) as we prepared to go on our honeymoon to Saskatoon and Regina. By the time we returned, I believe we were out of cash. We stopped in at Boissevain at my sister's place for the night, then went on to Niverville to visit another sister before settling into our home to face the new challenges before us.

We came back home to no well in the yard and no indoor plumbing; as a matter of fact, no outhouse! We had some help digging a well (about twelve feet deep, with a thirty-six-inch concrete casing), which gave us great water for the house and the animals.

The outhouse, well, that was another matter. I remember receiving visitors and having to tell them we had no outhouse, other than the same gutter the cattle used in the barn. Yes, it was embarrassing, but that was the start to our marriage. The day came when we found a solid "two-holer" outhouse, brought it home and dug a pit to set it on. Luxury at last!

Eleanor got a cow as a gift from her parents; a few months later, I was given a heifer, not a cow, from my parents because

I had not contributed my fair share to the family income. I got married too young! So, getting enough income off the rented farm would be tough, even though we had put in the crop in the spring with the help of my dad as well as Eleanor's dad.

The harvest was not the greatest; selling some crop and keeping the rest to feed the animals would not leave enough money to keep groceries on the table for winter. On one occasion, when I wanted to mail a letter, I gathered empty drink bottles along the road to buy a stamp. There was a very gracious couple, Sam and Ada Williams, who owned the Pine Creek Store where we could charge up groceries to keep us through the winter. The first year went by quickly, and to this day, I am still shocked that Eleanor put up with me and continued to be at my side, but I am thankful she did. It must have been love—or else it was a burning desire to get away from home that convinced her she should take this leap of faith!

That first year, we made the decision to go back to the EMC and make the church of our youth our home church. I recall the resulting conflict that arose. We would have been so much better off if we had stuck with what we wanted to do in the first place; my parents would have made the adjustment sooner.

Nine months after we were married, Eleanor became pregnant. Another nine months passed when, in January 1970, we went to visit my sister Kathy and her husband, George, in Niverville. By then, I had sold my 1962 Chevrolet and bought a rickety old 1953 Ford half-ton with the windows taped up to keep them closed. Niverville was a full two-hour trip in minus 30-degree Celsius temperatures with blowing snow! It was nine in the evening and time to head for home so we could get back before midnight. A fully due pregnant wife at my side, we left in the dark of night. My sister begged us to stay for the night, but nope, we had chores to do and animals to feed. So, off we went into the blinding snow. Not a bright idea, even today with all the advantages of better vehicles and communication devices!

Not much later, on a bitterly cold night in early February, we made the gruelling one-hour drive to the Portage Hospital and spent one night there. There was no opportunity to sit in the labour room, let alone the birthing room, so I was stuck in the hallway, waiting, only to be told the next morning that Eleanor's contractions had stopped and we could go home. On our way, we stopped briefly at a store for a few things. We needed to be ready to come back, she said, but this time she would wait till she was sure; she did not want to be embarrassed again. On February 4, after a full forty-eight hours in labour, Darryl, our firstborn, arrived—a gift to us to care for!

Meanwhile, the farm endeavour at Helston appeared to be a futile effort. Poor crops meant we were looking for other sources of income. The Canadian Wheat Board permit system was a bit of a joke, but it did give me opportunity to deliver grain based on the allowance on my permit, even if I didn't have enough of my own to fill my quota. I noticed Lee's Equipment in Brandon had put out an ad looking for half-tons, and they would pay for the truck with wheat instead of cash! I had purchased a Chevy half-ton and decided I could make some money off of it. My plan was to drop off the Chevy with the promise to deliver the purchased wheat to the elevator (under my name) and get the cash at a later date. I remember driving the truck to Brandon, making the deal for 1,200 bushels of wheat (way beyond what I thought the truck was worth) then hitch-hiking home from Brandon, hungry and not a dollar to my name.

Realizing this farming endeavour at Helston was a futile effort, we rented a farmyard from a Mrs. Smiley on Highway 34. Closer to civilization! We had some cattle, pigs, sheep and geese to look after; running water was still only available if we ran to the house from the well. We gave farming another shot that spring; however, success in farming was not to be. I could not pay my bills, and we had to move off the farm.

My brother-in-law, Henry Tiessen from Boissevain, had a turkey operation. While doing business with Glen Lawson from Clark's Poultry Farm and Hatchery in Brandon, he found out that Clark's needed an employee. Sight unseen, no interview, I went to Brandon to try out my new job. It was very simple. The breeding flock had been cleaned out, and I was responsible for removing a year's worth of manure out of this two-storey building one shovelful at a time! The job went well; hard work never scared me.

In the fall of 1970, while we were still trying to get rid of the last of the crop-failure bills, I moved my family, which now included Darryl, into a basement suite at 730 22nd Street in Brandon. It was a great move, but we never settled into a new church because we kept driving back to MacGregor every Sunday.

One thing I didn't do before we left the community of MacGregor was connect with the creditor from whom I had purchased my flaxseed for planting the spring of 1970. This was the very situation I had determined never to get into! Yet, there I was, lacking the nerve to acknowledge my intent to pay my bills. Since this creditor was a farmer who was on the church board, he made sure I was called before the church to address this issue. At the time, I felt slighted and even resentful. Why would someone with a lot of money take this poor guy before the church elders? I could have even quoted the Scripture about the one who had been forgiven much, then went out and extracted the last drop from someone who owed him a little bit! However, as I look back, I see there was in fact a very important lesson I needed to learn. I needed to face my inability to keep my commitment and acknowledge it to the people involved. Learning to be responsible and talk to others about my commitments left a lasting impression and impacted how I would do business and treat others in the future.

God provided a job for me where I could feed my family and start paying off my creditors. Bankruptcy never entered my mind. I had made a promise and I would keep it! I believe it was that same type of commitment that held Eleanor and me together as we discovered the pluses and minuses of married life, how one decision always leads to another and how it can impact much more than it seems at the time. Life became easier financially, but we could never allow circumstances in our lives to affect our marriage in any way, other than making a deeper commitment to work things out. I firmly believe that if we had married later in life and had gone through similar situations, our marriage would have fallen apart. A tree that does not bend breaks far sooner than a twig that is still pliable. Being teenagers, we didn't know better, and when the storms hit, we remained flexible.

Teenage Marriage

Martin and Eleanor at their wedding on August 4, 1968, eighteen and seventeen years old, respectively

A Scrappy Little Nobody

Martin and Eleanor's wedding

Sod turning for our first biffy outhouse in 1969

Our very adventurous second-eldest daughter, Lyndell

NINE:
Adapting to Circumstances

I could never have imagined the changes that lay before me as I started a new career in Brandon. My opportunities would be limitless, and my work ethic and self-discipline would now be the determining factors for future success. My responsibilities in the barn were short-lived, as I transitioned to working in the hatchery as well as the Grand Valley egg station. I had the opportunity to take baby chicks from the incubators and practise distinguishing between males and females with super speed and accuracy! We were able to process 10,000 to 15,000 chicks in a single day, sexing them one at a time with 99 percent accuracy. That process involved disposing of all the males because it would cost more in feed to raise the leghorn males than they would be worth. On the job, I continued to learn the health risks of these pullets, particularly their tendency to peck each other to death if they were not "debeaked." That became my job. To remove the tip, I stuck each beak into a small hole, just big enough to take off the right portion, then stepped on a lever that would chop off the beak with a searing hot knife.

The poultry industry was facing a huge challenge dealing with Marek's disease (fowl paralysis). That meant a vaccine had to be injected very precisely under the skin of every chicken's neck. I got pretty good at these tasks and learned the poultry industry from the ground up as I had done with most things I accomplished. I do have to admit, I got the odd jab that entered my own finger! As I learned the fundamentals of bird husbandry, I was given the opportunity to go out on customer service and sales calls. This took me on the road connecting with poultry farmers across Manitoba, including many Hutterites. These opportunities set the stage for a yet unforeseen future career. After two years of spending more time on the road than in the hatchery, Eleanor and I decided that it might be better to move out of Brandon and back to the Austin/Sidney area to a farmyard where we could earn additional income by raising piglets. It also meant I saved a lot of miles, as most of our customers were in Eastern Manitoba. We were back among friends and closer to our home church. The next two years were spent on the road, building customer relations and, as planned, beginning a secondary income by raising piglets.

* * *

During this season of life, my faith was enriched and grew. The conservative church I was raised in taught that good works were very much counted as a credit in God's books, as were my experiences with giving. I recall growing up and seeing the church leaders come by my parents' farm every fall "collecting" church fees. It was always a dreaded time, from what I recall, and my dad would not look forward to the visit. Putting down my own spiritual roots and seeking to be a voluntary generous giver, I sought the Scriptures that supported the idea of tithing. The term was familiar to me in theory but certainly not followed in practice. I committed to God that I would be faithful in obeying this precept going forward. Giving from a paycheque was easier, but when I purchased ten bred sows, intending to sell the weanlings, giving ten percent of the end income would prove to be much more difficult. I was fortunate to have a very good herd, producing a wonderful crop of healthy weanlings, and then fortunate to also have good buyers.

You would think I would remember the word that says in Deuteronomy 26:10 (NIV), "… and now I bring the first fruits of the soil that you, O Lord, have given me …" And Malachi 3:10 talks about bringing the tithe or first fruits to the storehouse "'… that there may be food in my house. Test me in this,' says the Lord Almighty, 'and see if I will not throw open the floodgates of heaven and pour out so much blessing that you will not have room enough room for it.'" I needed to learn another lesson. I had nine sows with weanlings that I sold, paid the bills, spent the rest on myself and forgot my commitment to God. I recall clearly the day that the last sow, which had the biggest and best litter at the outset, was subsequently hit with mastitis and every one of her weanlings died.

I cried out to God, "Why? This was the one tenth I promised you!"

Today, approximately fifty years later, what I heard from God is still as clear as the day it was revealed to me. "Martin, this was not mine; I don't work off of leftovers. If you love me, you will honour me with your first fruits."

I have never supported the prosperity Gospel and still don't, but I learned a very important truth from God. He deserves the first of my earnings, and I need to place Him and my offerings to Him in the right perspective. I have never forgotten that life lesson and I've adhered to it until this day. I don't expect immediate repayment and I don't get it. But I have learned to rely on God for everything I have, including each day I live, because He owns everything I have and has simply entrusted it to my care. It is with this in mind that I look at my career and life in general as a gift from God.

Adapting to Circumstances

In 1973, I had an opportunity to be employed by the MacGregor Co-op, where I started as a Hoover washer repair man. It would mean less time on the road and more time with family, and I would take on the role as a youth leader in our church. Life was great. Our second child, Lyndell, was added to our family; the new job at MacGregor Co-op quickly became a job in the fertilizer side of the business; and I was back to serving farmers! The co-op system was somewhat foreign to me, as I certainly was a "free entrepreneur" type of person. In less than a year, a local individual by the name of Dan Doell, who was employed by National Grain at an elevator in Firdale, Manitoba, decided he was leaving the grain business. I had never met him, but he was aware of my existence, so he informed his boss that perhaps he should speak to me about a job in the elevator. Well, this elevator was only three miles from our home and paid more money, and I could be home for lunch! That job interview went well, and I landed the position of elevator manager, even though I had barely set foot in an elevator my whole life! My co-op days were over and a new venture had begun.

With nothing to offer, other than my commitment to learn, I started my new career in February 1974. The elevator had no electrical connection other than lights in the office. Everything else was 100 percent driven off a single-cylinder diesel stationary engine by shafts, cable and ropes. My first day on the job was a Monday and the retired former manager, Albert Manns, was to be there to help me learn the "ropes." I showed up, but no Albert, so how could I start this thing? After switching many levers, exhausting all the air in the start-up cylinder, I attempted to start it by hand. I couldn't even get it to push the cylinder to the point of firing because I didn't know the compression in the engine could be reduced. After hours of trying, with trucks lined up in the driveway, I finally figured it out and got it going! Lesson learned, never to be forgotten; the school of hard knocks was alive and well.

Just as I got into the swing of the business, I learned that a huge multinational grain company called Cargill had purchased National Grain. I thought my career would be short-lived; as this company had so many well-trained and educated people, I was sure to lose my job. I was shocked to find out that, no, they would help train me! Again, my career path continued to evolve, and God continued to supply all my needs.

Many customers appreciated my services, and by the fall of 1974, they were asking if we didn't want to purchase the Manitoba Pool elevator in Sidney. I suggested that, since I was employed at the elevator for less than a year, that decision would not be something I could influence. I was proven wrong again. I brought the idea to my boss, Gerry Lush, thinking nothing would happen, only to find out a short time later, they made a swap deal with the pool, trading a Northern elevator to the pool for Sidney! Within a few short weeks, I was to manage both the Sidney and Firdale elevators—all this after being employed there for less than a year.

My first experience handling rapeseed came at a cost. I purchased some number 3 grade in winter from Nelson Hulme in MacGregor, but I didn't know that the grain needed to be rotated in the bins. I discovered that one day. It was hot, and not wanting the elevator to burn down, I opened the bottom manhole entry, thinking the grain would simply spill over the floor and I would clean it up. But as I opened the bin at the bottom, nothing flowed. Nothing moved even after opening a two-foot square hole! Panic set in. I grabbed a field sprayer hitch support bar, dragged it to the top of the bin, got in and began poking into the grain. The rapeseed was so hot I could not stand in the bin! Eventually I poked it from the bottom and literally chipped away one piece at a time to get it to circulate. It never did, because it had the texture of a sugar cube. I am very fortunate that I did not lose my life in that bin. Again, only because of God's protection did I survive. Shortly after that ordeal, I became the manager at Sidney, and I hired my brother-in-law (who would help me take in the grain) as an interim assistant for Firdale. He also helped chisel out the rest of the rapeseed, and I believe he decided, right then and there, that was not the job he wanted!

The whirlwind of change continued. I gained experience selling farm supplies as I sat listening to farmers talk about their farming practices and the chemicals they used. I learned the difference between 2,4-D; MCPA; and Buctril M as well as their strengths. Then I gave advice to the customer needing help, based on what I heard. Coffee was always on and listening to the farmers' stories during "class" was very helpful. This opportunity to learn from others and hear their wise counsel helped develop my career in many facets in later years.

When I moved from operating the Firdale elevator to managing both the Firdale and Sidney elevators, we incorporated the use of a CB radio with antenna to reach the farmers and coordinate grain deliveries. We also pioneered the services of a custom fertilizer and chemical application with a Big A—which was actually a Terra Gator, a three-wheel truck. We also bought an Easy Rider, which was similar but somewhat different. The Easy Rider was a huge truck mount machine. These additions allowed us to charge for our services and, obviously, sell more farm input supplies.

The Sidney addition was highly profitable. I recall the first week after taking over the Sidney location; I handled more grain in that week than the previous manager handled in an entire year! I was on the front page of local print media both for the introduction of custom application as well as the introduction of CB radio as a marketing tool. I would relay the grain prices and so on regularly, and the farmers loved it!

Becoming successful meant surrounding myself with good people. While playing baseball on a local Sidney scrub team I hired two great guys by the name of Dale Rands and George Wieler. Both would prove to be great hires and were a tremendous asset as time went on.

The thing I loved about Cargill was that they allowed me to be unique, create opportunities and use my skills to the best advantage. I was supported as they added a new annex to that facility and expanded the farm supply business to include sunflowers. When those seeds came off in late October to early November, I was open twenty-four hours a day, napping between some loads! The farmers were so appreciative, at times they would unload their own seeds directly into the railcars standing on the track to support my lack of capacity. Besides, why elevate it twice?

On one occasion, I had ten grain cars being loaded with sunflowers to ship to Thunder Bay. I watched for unload results to show up, and one car never showed up as being unloaded. Months later, I was informed that the car never had any sunflowers in it—not a trace! It appears my night shift (me) was so busy moving cars, one slipped by empty! The weight was estimated, so I never realized this happened till months later. Well, both my employer and the railway thought this was so humorous that the railway eliminated the freight bill for that car!

There are dozens of other stories (some not that funny) of incidents that could have resulted in me being fired. But, because I was dedicated to the job and built relationships, not only with farmers but with the movers and shakers of Cargill, I was given the chance to learn the skills needed. Roger Murray, the president of Cargill, and Bill Neilson, the vice-president, would frequently come to the elevator to see how it was going.

In addition, I was given the opportunity to sell Zipperlock buildings, a company that Bill owned, along with a trucking company.

The second year at Sidney, when the president and vice-president stopped by, I was wearing a Zipperlock hat. Roger was not impressed, and words were exchanged between the two after they left. Roger questioned why I was not wearing a Cargill hat; Bill informed him I could wear a Cargill hat working for Zipperlock if he preferred that! Nothing more was ever said about my hat choices, and in fact, one year I earned more money from Zipperlock than Cargill. That was the year I got an offer to take my family to Disney World, all expenses paid! I got the gift and never found out if it came from Cargill or Zipperlock—and I never asked.

My relationships with people and my motivation in the private sector proved my value as an entrepreneur; as an employee, it placed me in good standing with the company, which would help in difficult times. In 1978, I was promoted to area manager for Southwest Manitoba and bought a brand-new Pontiac Parisienne Brougham.

One bitterly cold morning, I proceeded to Sidney to the office. I was approaching a railway intersection, and on my left, the tracks were somewhat obscured. The icy crossing was very slippery. When I heard the whistle blow, I realized, too late, a train was coming! Decision time ... abandon the car, tramp it or try to stop on the ice? In a split second, I stepped on the gas, the car swerved and the back bumper landed square in the path of the oncoming train, which hit the car, bouncing me some one hundred feet off the tracks!

It took the conductor a mile to stop the train; all the while he was thinking, *Fatality!* My new car looked like an A-frame, a total write-off. But, again, by God's grace and mercy on me, I stepped out of it untouched, without a scratch. The relief on the train engineer's face when he ran back to the accident was amazing!

Calling my wife felt like a miracle in itself. I was again reminded of the brevity of life. At best, my life hung in the balance of God's mercy as He continued to shape and prepare me for what He saw my future would hold.

TEN:
Life's Surprises

Life continued at a very rapid pace. Eleanor and I were involved in our church. We now had a son and a daughter. We had friends. In 1978, we built a new home just north of Sidney, secluded in thirteen acres of bush land cleared and developed, with a well and sewage septic system. We were finally set to live a normal life and enjoy it.

January 1, 1979, was a beautiful, cold, sunshiny day with a bit of snow falling from time to time. We celebrated New Year's Day (no alcohol) with our friends Bill and Sharon as well as Eleanor's brother, Birnie, and his wife, Wanda. The guys decided to venture out into the hills for a ride on our snowmobiles. For some reason, I couldn't generate enough speed on my machine to keep up; as I struggled, I noticed Bill and Birnie quite a distance ahead at the bottom of a slope, waiting for me to catch up. Finally getting the machine wound up, I decided I would pass them, then ride it all the way to the peak of the ridge ahead. What I did not see was that a huge snow drift had created a solid wall straight up to the crest. I hit that wall at top speed—it must have looked like a scene from a stunt movie—making it all the way up to the top of the hill, with Bill and Birnie cheering ... but there was nothing to cheer about. The windshield of the snowmobile had come up, hit my chin, loosened my bottom four teeth and knocked off the top four at the roots! There I was, spitting teeth and blood all over the fresh white snow. The fun was over.

Riding home, I found out what exposed nerves felt like. We were about six miles from our friends' place and the cold winter air stung. The temperature was so cold that the bleeding had stopped, but the pain was unreal! The gash on my chin was wide enough for me to stick my tongue through, and I had no top teeth! I went to the emergency in MacGregor looking for medical attention only to be given pain killers and told to see a dentist. The next day was Monday of a long weekend, and I would have to wait till Tuesday to get help. When I looked at my injured chin, I quickly realized, one inch lower and the windshield would have completely severed my jugular vein.

Come Tuesday, I was off to Brandon to see the dentist, who had only one piece of advice: if capping was not affordable, remove what was left of the top four teeth and eventually get a partial plate. That was all well and good, but in two weeks, we were going to Florida for our free Disney World trip! No front teeth, staying at a very luxurious hotel with what looked like celebrities (judging by the fancy cars) and gumming it. All my pride was gone.

Though I tried to hide my face while walking in public areas, my family and I still enjoyed the two-week trip. For Darryl, a fun new life experience awaited. He was nine and had the opportunity to ride on the Batmobile boat with Batman. He loved it and remembers that event like it was yesterday. (After what I had recently gone through, I have no idea why Eleanor and I signed the waiver; I have to attribute that decision to being a "risk taker.")

For me, the New Year's Day adventure was another experience that I chalk up to God's grace in my life, His provision and the assurance of His presence protecting and preparing

Life's Surprises

me for what lay ahead. This was episode number four of what could potentially have been an end-of-life experience, but God was not done yet; a long life was still ahead for me.

In the spring of 1979, six years after our daughter Lyn arrived in answer to our fervent prayers, the Lord brought Rhonda into our lives. She was such a blessing and a gift! With Rhonda's arrival, Eleanor and I had met our objective of having three kids by the time we were thirty years old. We wanted to be young enough to enjoy them and still be able to enjoy life after they grew up. In hindsight, seeing how our life story unfolded, we were grateful we did.

Eleanor was a very hardworking homemaker. She loved our family and the Lord and was a diligent, caring mom to our kids. Besides being very supportive in my career moves, she served in the ladies' ministry and singing groups, and helped out in my ministry. We had a busy year with weekly youth meetings at our home and in church, along with a church building project. Life was normal, or so it seemed.

The following winter, we had occasion to represent Cargill at community agriculture and sports events. As area manager, I was involved in the oversight of four new elevator builds in my territory: Brandon, Rivers, Tenby and Newdale as a start. The business went great; the fertilizer and custom application business boomed. But that meant more was in store ahead.

One day, I received a call from my boss, Curt Vossen, asking if Eleanor and I would be able to attend a minor hockey league banquet in Morris. His excuse for not wanting to attend himself was that he was not married and that we, as a couple, would be a better fit for the event. I questioned that. I really had little interest in hockey and it was totally out of my sales area. But, attend we did, and after the weekend, I got a call disclosing the real reason for this request to attend the game.

"What did you think of Morris?" he asked me.

Well, other than almost dying there as a baby, I really didn't have an opinion.

"How would you like to move there to run a new elevator we are planning on building there?"

What could I say, other than I would speak to Eleanor to discuss it. I did talk to her, and wanting to support her husband, she agreed we should move.

The following week, I got another call. Something had come up in Winkler; the existing manager at that location had been removed and they "needed" me to step in. Cargill had already established a presence there by purchasing the special crops plant from Kroeker Farms. I had no idea what had gone wrong at the Winkler elevator. Cargill was now in the process of adding a new elevator to handle grain and was getting into the fertilizer and chemical business.

My response was immediate. "Nope, not interested." When my parents sold the farm and contemplated moving to Winkler, I had decided that was the last place I would move to.

That day, I made my way home and explained to Eleanor what I had said, thinking she would be ecstatic about not having to move to Winkler, but she surprised me.

"Why not?" she said. "At least we already know some people that go there to visit." So, I called Curt Vossen back and told him we would accept the offer.

That was an interesting "move." Be there Monday morning, rent a hotel room at the Winkler Inn, work during the week and come home for weekends. In the meantime, look for a house and get ready to physically move the family to Winkler.

I honestly knew no one, other than one cousin and his wife, Peter and Lottie Harder, but we had lost touch with each other. While looking for a house, our first adventure took place on Ascension Day when we quickly discovered a difference between local Mennonite cultural practices and our earlier communities. Ascension Day (a church holiday celebrated worldwide to commemorate Christ's ascension into heaven) always falls on the Thursday forty days after Easter Sunday. In Winkler, all the stores, including real estate offices, were closed. We finally found an agent who was willing to take us around to see some properties for just a drive by. We wanted to live in the country, not in town, so that's where we looked. Our first impression of Winkler did not come with a lot of positive vibes, as we were not familiar with the conservative lifestyle that we saw.

Travelling south of Winkler, we discovered a small group of homes along Highway 32 in Little Schanzenfeld. What drew us back later to take another look was seeing some people with bathing suits on, enjoying the sunshine! Now we were interested. In fact, we went back to look at the home beside the place where we had seen the person in a bathing suit, and yep, we bought it. The price was of similar value to our current home's estimated worth, so it was financially possible. On a humorous note, we'd been told we had a lot of relatives in and around Winkler, but little did we know that the couple next door actually were my second cousins! They were awesome neighbours, became great friends—*bring a friend, be a friend*—and stood by our family through difficult times. This experience proved once again, don't judge a book by its cover ... or evaluate a community based on a drive-by viewing. Regardless of others' opinions, including our own preconceived notions, we had a positive experience.

Moving to Winkler did not mean a salary increase. I have never in my life needed to negotiate salary levels and I have never had disagreements regarding salaries. I always felt I would be paid what I was worth while having my needs recognized. I can't say that I always deserved what I got, but now I experienced it again. Similar to my comment about being a friend, being a great employee and giving my best has worked very well for me and has contributed to the many opportunities I was given.

Working for Cargill, I was employed by a company that was loved by many but also hated by those who simply argued against the existence of any private multinational corporation, regardless of the strengths they brought to agriculture. In my experience, because I lacked formal education, being a high school drop-out, the company stepped up to provide me with all the courses I needed to do a better job. They equipped me to be able to manage "my business" because that is the decision-making power I was given. It was not because of my education but because of a proven track record that I was given the privilege of learning so I could perform my best. My courses included learning people skills, sales techniques, leadership skills, safety performance, account collection skills. Later in my career, I participation in designing a new computer business management system, not as a programmer, but testing the practical ease and functionality of the system. The ability to write annual budgets was critical, and being held accountable for those numbers was drilled into me. That became a key asset for my future as it continued to evolve.

I was also given the privilege of training young university agriculture graduates to become great grain traders and future vice-presidents of Cargill. Wow, what an honour to have such a huge support network among the Cargill group, whom I credit to this day with preparing me for ongoing future opportunities. Again, and again I realized the value of people and the importance of never burning bridges, but rather, building on experiences that could take me to the next level. I will forever be grateful for these and many more opportunities afforded to me by this great company, Cargill Grain.

Life's Surprises

* * *

On the other hand, getting settled in Winkler was difficult. We had decided on the house in Schanzenfeld as a place to live, but we struggled with how to make connections in our new surroundings. Winkler had many very successful farmers; possibly, I could have made the best contacts by going to a large church attended by farmers. We struggled with that but knew in our hearts that success does not come from using the church to make you prosperous. We made a commitment to God that we would not use a Sunday church service to promote business. It was our place of refuge, intended to build up our faith and nurture our spiritual growth. And that is how we ended up in a church on 3rd Street South, the smallest church in Winkler, attended by approximately sixty people—and not one farmer. It was not the easy way out, but it was the right way, and God rewarded that commitment. The process for building connections took longer, but the quality of those connections was better.

I was encouraged by my employer to get involved in the community. My right-hand man, Dale Rands, and I both enjoyed playing on the Reinfeld baseball team, and we got to know people that way. At work, while the downtown street was lined up with trucks waiting for the pool elevator to unload their grain, Dale and I would play catch on the Cargill elevator driveway, waiting for trucks. I had to remind my boss that I was not looking for a quick fix. I was there to establish a dependable customer base, and my employers had patience. Eventually, it worked.

I had been asked to work at the new terminal in Elm Creek in 1978 and again in 1983. When I asked my boss if I was pretty permanent at Winkler, I was assured "Yes." However, a month after I had poured the foundation of a living room addition to our house, I was asked to go to Elm Creek again. The manager, Gerald McElroy, had suffered a major heart attack and passed away, leaving an opening for director of operations at Elm Creek. Not wanting to relocate my family, and at the risk of losing my job, I said, "No." My boss did not like to be turned down. I kept my job, although communication with Cargill management was pretty cool for a while.

In 1984, I became president of the Winkler and District Chamber of Commerce, opening up a whole new avenue of experience. In 1985, we celebrated the grand opening of the Southland Mall. At the same time, Old Time Value Days in Winkler transitioned to become the Harvest Festival at a new site in the northwest corner of Winkler. Tickets were sold for a Ford Thunderbird giveaway, with revenue going to help cover the festival costs. The big star American singer Ronnie Millsap would be brought in, more tickets would be sold and Winkler would be on the map!

Well, not so fast. The rain came down. The performance was all but drowned out, and there were more people standing around the outside of the ticketed fence than inside. Disaster had struck! Now what to do? As Chamber president, I did not want to leave a blemish hanging around Winkler. Technically, the festival did not report to the Chamber, but Alvin Thiessen, who was on the board of the Harvest Festival (and a major retail business owner operating Economy Foods), met with me to figure out a solution. The rest of the members had scattered, leaving it up to us to meet with creditors, bankers and city council to get to a solution. We successfully negotiated our bill to the bare minimum, in particular with our major creditor, Harvey Friesen from the *Winkler Times*. Town council, along with Mayor Henry F. Wiebe, consented to extend an additional grant. We approached the Scotiabank in Winkler and borrowed a further $30,000 with personal guarantees to cover the rest of the bills.

In 1986, I offered to run the Winkler Harvest Festival. In three years, we had the loan paid off, with enough money in the account to pay for a new stage and seating area. The festival continues to be a major summer event in the Valley. Again, not burning bridges, but working with the people who make a difference in Winkler continues to be the answer!

ELEVEN:
When Love and Marriage Meet Life's Realities

Since I have always been involved in "side business" ventures, I've had a tough time deciphering personal versus business venture finance. In the corporate world, I had someone else looking after those details and didn't worry about the finer accounting issues. There were others with those skills. My job was to look after the big picture, to look into the future, discern a vision and make it happen.

As we settled in Winkler, more mundane opportunities came along. We noticed many homes had been neglected when it came to upkeep. Inside some of them, you couldn't breathe because smoke from cigarettes had penetrated the Gyproc walls. Buying dilapidated houses, fixing them up and reselling them seemed like a great business on the side. I started with one house at a time, purchasing on thin finances and operating loans. Sometimes I had early possession and got some work done before I actually had to pay for the house. It appeared I was making money; however, I did not keep track of my personal use of that account or how much money I was spending on other personal wants.

I had a method of accounting that many people understand: it's called "shoebox accounting." Receipts are kept in a shoebox, and when it comes to filing taxes, you simply bring the box to the person doing the returns and they'll figure it out. It started with a friend of a friend who had done their tax returns and he was cheap, so that's where I took my shoebox. The friend of my shoebox and the banker handling my bank account never met. So, there was a bit of a disconnect. Nevertheless, there was always more money to spend, and since we had an operating loan at the bank, there was no need to reconcile the two. I had used this method for years, even before we moved to Winkler (which likely explains why I did not survive being a farmer at the beginning of our marriage). Credit card debt was under control. I always had a fetish for paying bills on time, and I detested paying high interest to credit card companies. Having an operating line of credit was certainly the lesser evil.

This went on for several years, and one day, Eleanor and I decided we needed to separate business expenses from personal expenses and keep track of our spending. With the sale of the last project home, the operating line would be fully paid off. Well, the chickens came home to roost, but the nest was empty; we still had an operating line of credit of close to $10,000. The day of reckoning had arrived, and it was time to balance the account. It took some time and discipline to pay off the loan. I was grateful that I had a good job with a steady income so paying off this debt was not a huge burden to my family.

Now a number of changes needed to take place. I put Eleanor in charge of the bank account to balance expenses and start a better personal financing and bookkeeping process. We had some fun chatting about what our financial picture looked like and decided our marriage needed to be a balanced affair. My job was to supply the income; Eleanor's job was to ensure it was spent! Truthfully, she was very meticulous and always looked like a model; now she backed up her reputation for being particular by using her skills in managing our bank account. That was the beginning of getting on track financially.

For some reason, Canada Revenue Agency couldn't quite figure out what was happening with our finances, as there was a lot of money flowing but very little showing up on the bottom line. One day, we had a call from the CRA requesting to see my bank account records as well as my "book work." So, I brought them my shoeboxes for the years they asked for, including all my bank statements and paycheque records. I knew fairly well where my income came from and where it went, but my record keeping left one wondering just how it was done. Up to that point, keeping all my records in shoeboxes had served me very well.

After the CRA disallowed my property-flipping revenue as a capital gain—I would need to declare it as income—it appeared I would owe them a significant amount of money. Then I had another call asking for a receipt for a particular deposit, claiming I had not included it in that year's income. As my shoebox accounting went, it was impossible to come up with that specific deposit for that specific year. The amount looked familiar; it looked like a bonus cheque or perhaps a tax refund, and I was fairly consistent in making both of those deposits with a degree of regularity. Giving was a way of life for us, so there was usually a tax refund, and since my employment income included bonuses, that was an annual occurrence as well. This should not be hard! Eleanor and I spent an entire evening and into the wee hours of the morning rummaging through my shoeboxes to no avail. We would have to pay this bill if we couldn't find the required income receipt for that year.

Finally, I looked more closely at the auditor's request and saw that he had listed that particular deposit in the wrong year—and he wanted me to prove I had the records! Once we were on the same page (or year), I immediately recognized the amount as a bonus deposit clearly included in the year I earned it. To my credit, my shoebox accounting had won the day! All the same, I was not happy. The next morning, I met the auditor at the hotel where he was staying to do the audit. We exchanged some unpleasantries about how incompetent he was, and that was the end of the audit. I had learned a valuable lesson about the importance of good recordkeeping, as well as recognizing that in the future I needed a better bookkeeper.

As is usually the case, there was a bill owing, including penalties for previous years, because they disallowed the capital gains process. Since the CRA insisted on using the business income model, in their books, I had also made significant investments. For example, I had purchased a house from my brother-in-law that might have gone into bank repossession. The deal was that I would buy it and fix it up, and eventually, as he was able, he would buy it back from me. All was fine and because it was family, I didn't want to include that in my expense column. Since the CRA wanted "all" my dealings, I appealed their decision and included the family venture, which meant I actually received an adjustment and a refund after the audit. This reinforced my decision to be much more careful about keeping proper records and to hire not only a good bookkeeper but also a great accountant.

From that year onward, we kept our personal and business finances separate, paying the accountant's dues to cover my shortfalls. In time, I was able to assist others in their business decisions and help them avoid similar circumstances. Sometimes it worked; other times they needed to discover these principles on their own. The fundamental changes that Eleanor and I made because of this experience were invaluable for managing any endeavours that would come in the future.

A Scrappy Little Nobody

My dad, George (age eighty); my mom, Anna (eighty); Martin (forty); Darryl (twenty); and my youngest, Rhonda (ten), playing double-double!

When Love and Marriage Meet Life's Realities

Martin and Eleanor on mid-1980s date night

Martin at brother Don and wife Audrey's home for an extended Harder sibling reunion in Ontario

TWELVE:
Family Values and Lessons Learned

One week before Thanksgiving, I was driving down Highway 32 and there, in the ditch, sat a turkey, stunned but very much alive. I stopped by the side of the road to load it into my trunk, and later dropped by a youth event at our church to show the kids. What to do with this bird? Since Thanksgiving was around the corner, I considered it God's gift to our family and took it home. Well, the whole neighbourhood came over to watch this turkey being prepared for our Thanksgiving dinner! It may have freaked out some kids who had never experienced butchering a turkey, but it became a new community event. I assumed this fine feathered bird riding on the back of a truck loaded with other docile turkeys chose to spring a cage and, as sometimes happens, ended up dumbfounded on the side of the road, only to become a delicious turkey dinner on our family table.

* * *

In comparison to the issues families face today, raising a son and two daughters in the 1970s to 1990s should have been easy. It was a time with no Twitter, TikTok or Facebook,

A Scrappy Little Nobody

and TV viewing was very limited. There was a lot of time for kids to play outdoors with a dog and cats, pets that were not allowed in the house. Our kids had opportunities to take music lessons, each of them according to their interests. Darryl learned guitar, Lyn played piano, and Rhonda took both violin and piano lessons. I found it curious that the violin teacher discouraged Rhonda from taking lessons, saying her wrists were too stiff and she did not overarch the bow correctly. Their weekly routine included regular attendance at youth nights, church and Sunday school. To give them a firm foundation when facing future life challenges, we offered all three children free tuition for their first year of Bible school after high school graduation. The girls took us up on it, but it seemed they both chose a school as far away from home as they could imagine. Lyn chose to go to Australia to a Capernwray Bible School, and Rhonda chose to go to Capernwray in Sweden. Both were short-term programs, but at least they learned the values and disciplines we adhered to. Darryl preferred to stay close to home and never ventured out; that was his choice.

We did not have a TV in every room. As a matter of principle, we never allowed a TV in any bedrooms, including our own. The shows our children watched were geared to "family friendly" entertainment—*MASH* and *Bonanza* were as violent as it got. The value of the Bible and the truth of that content was accepted and, by and large, appreciated in our society at that time. Our core friends and families adhered to and supported those same values, and found our home to be a very accepting and inviting environment. For our kids' friends, as well as neighbourhood kids wanting to enjoy some fun time with them, it was Central Station. Generally, the girls were open to having their playmates over and chose to stay home rather than go to others' places. That changed as they entered their teen years. In 1985, after the Southland Mall was built in

Winkler, they hung out with friends there. Occasionally, for entertainment purposes and obviously shopping, Eleanor and I would be at the mall at the same time as our teenage daughter Lyn. Some of those days were a bit tough as Mom and Dad hanging around the mall while she was there with her "crowd" was *not appreciated*. As far as our middle child was concerned, Dad knew *very little*.

Those were the days when curfew was a part of family rules but not high on the list of things that were appreciated. Lyn, especially, seemed somewhat discontent, and she repeatedly ignored or stretched her curfew time. One evening, thoroughly exasperated by her habitually pushing the boundaries, we adjusted her curfew from 11:00 p.m. to 10:00 p.m. to help her get back on track. Well, she was a girl who needed everything explained to her liking. Needless to say, that did not bode well for either of us, because on this occasion, I was done explaining. I very plainly informed her the reason her mother and I were adjusting her curfew was that we were simply tired and needed her home before we went to bed. I know that may seem odd, but to us, loving our kids meant that we cared who they hung out with and what time they arrived back home.

One evening, as we were discussing the need for curfew, we were "advised" that our best friend's daughter, with whom Lyn occasionally hung out, actually had *no* curfew. We double-checked with her parents to see if that was true and quickly found out it was fabricated, either by Lyn or her friend, who may have tried the same line on her parents as well. We were used to other kids coming to our place. To suddenly not see them and to have our daughter out with "who knows who" was a new experience.

Lyn was usually not afraid to try new things; she was a bit adventurous. On a day that proved to be fatal for her cat, she was in a hurry and quickly backed the car out of a parking spot without looking first to see where the feline was. The telling bump under the tire and then having her brother come to take care of the remains seems to have left an indelible impact on her. Today she lives in a home with multiple cats and dogs, some goats and chickens. While we were visiting her recently, she was on her way to work—she is a music professional overseeing a conservatory of music and also works full time as a church administrator—when she unexpectedly showed up back at the farm carrying a little dog in her arms. Not knowing what to do with it, she took the dog to work with her and enquired about the owner of the dog, only to be informed that the poor animal belonged to the neighbour from whose driveway she had rescued/abducted it! Not much later (after we returned home from our visit) and again on her way to work, she noticed what she thought was a puppy floundering in the creek close to their farm. Undeterred by the cold water and determined to rescue the puppy, she jumped into the creek. She barely got herself out of the water when she discovered the "puppy" was actually a possum, and clearly possums could swim very well! When I heard this sequel to the other story, I realized that we had raised a caring daughter who loves animals, and had an even deeper love for her family and friends. What a gift our family has been blessed with!

After Lyn got married, she had teens of her own who developed a behavioural pattern similar to their mother's when she was a teen. One day, I got a phone call from Lyn at her home in Texas.

"Dad," she said, "you remember when you told me the reason I needed to be home was because you were tired? Well, last night, I told my teenager the same thing!"

I was comforted then, knowing not all was lost, and yes, perhaps Mom and Dad were not so very odd after all. As I found out later, we'd had good reason at the time to be concerned.

It wasn't till 2022 that Lyn was finally brave enough to tell me, "Dad, do you remember the flowers under my bedroom window and how they struggled to survive? Well, I admit that, at the expense of those flowers, I crawled out of that window after curfew to go for another ride with my friends."

* * *

Our kids all enjoyed a weekly allowance, with chores to match the paycheque. It was a lesson in responsibility, and we expected them to contribute a portion of their allowance to the offering plate in Sunday school. In most cases that went well. I do remember a day when Darryl had bigger eyes than the contents of his pocket book and decided to spend his allowance on candy and a magazine. As he came back to the car, I asked him if he had remembered his money for the offering. He realized he had not and quickly returned to the store to return an item so he had his offering money left. I don't want to belabour the importance of learning that God deserves the first portion of the offering. I trust that those lessons we taught our kids early in their lives will not be forgotten.

Darryl was a bit shyer than our girls, so his friend list was a little shorter. He made good friends who didn't seem to lead him too far off track. The day we moved to Winkler, when the moving truck rolled up, there was a welcoming group of kids at the end of our driveway waiting for their new neighbours so they could introduce themselves. We had to almost force our son to go meet these kids! Darryl was a "home boy," who enjoyed loud music and playing bass guitar. During his teen years, we renovated a basement room to accommodate his need for privacy and personal space. To help with soundproofing, we placed a rug around the walls of his room to absorb the noise; it helped a lot. Darryl also loved cars and was privileged to experience many different models. They all had one thing in common: the sound had to be perfect. Once he got into cars, it was most important that the car had a "boom box" that rivalled, if not exceeded, the value of the car. When it came to his curfew, Darryl was pretty punctual. In fact, the neighbours would know from a quarter mile away how conscientious he was because all they heard was *boom, boom, boom* as he approached the service road going past our house. Even they were comforted, knowing he had arrived home safely.

Rhonda, our youngest, had a special attachment to her mom and that was clearly evident for a long time. When Rhonda was a year and a half old, Eleanor sang with a ladies' group; throughout singing practice, Rhonda was stuck to Eleanor's hip, clinging to her like a wet blanket. As she grew up, our earlier restrictions seemed to have become a bit more relaxed, and it appeared that Rhonda had way more privileges than her two older siblings. I am not sure if she recognized this herself, but it was true. She would regularly have friends over, including some kids belonging to our neighbours. Generally, they got along very well, except for the youngest, who was particularly whiney whenever things didn't go her way. One day, I stepped outside to advise her that if she didn't quit screaming whenever she didn't get her way, she would not be allowed to jump on our trampoline anymore. I never heard her cry at our place again, but she did come to play.

We had some very good friends in the Toews families and spent a lot of time together. At Abe and Sadie Toews' place, Rhonda had no one to play with; still, she was very content just to be there. When she was tired, she'd lay down and go to sleep quite comfortably on their bed. She had a good internal clock and could fall sleep anywhere. In time, Rhonda's life took on the role of compassionate listener. She is tender-hearted and sensitive, characteristics shown by the empathy she demonstrates for every hurting heart. Her family is of greatest value to her, and she will do everything possible to ensure those relationships remain intact.

As a family, we enjoyed special trips together: fishing trips as well as trips to Florida Disney World, California and Mazatlán, Mexico. Family times were so important, and Eleanor and I were very grateful for our wonderful family. As time went on, this included the three additional members our kids chose as life partners. Lyn connected with her future husband Jon in her semester break, while at Capernwray in Australia. Rhonda had been dating Steve previously before she left for Sweden, however a strained relationship put that on hold, until they both returned home on the same flight from Europe. Capernwray was an answer to our prayers for both girls, and their future choices. Darryl chose an internet dating site and found an awesome mate in Guasave, Mexico. I believe that, for someone never wanting to leave home, it was God who provided a way for Darryl and Dina to meet. Both are dedicated to serving God, and they are blessed with two grown children. Being open to God's leading in life opens up opportunities we could not have imagined.

Birthdays and wedding anniversaries are worth celebrating. In our home, they were always great family events with friends and family getting together. In time, due to her health, Eleanor didn't always feel up to a party, but she always took time for our kids and grandkids and made them feel special.

* * *

Once a place I was determined never to recommend, Winkler became something I could never have experienced anywhere else—a place where true, deep friendships were formed that lasted a lifetime. The smaller church setting without the familiar farming element allowed us to experience and process our own real-life issues; when we struggled, or our friends struggled, these true relationships came to the forefront. Church involvement became important again, with Eleanor serving as the ladies' group leader and getting involved in a neighbourhood women's Bible study group. These were the early days of my participation in the local economy and politics, and it ignited in me a deep desire to get more involved in community issues.

Though our family unit was close, Eleanor and I seemed distant from each other. My life was busy, which left very little time for building or supporting a strong marriage. The success I experienced as a builder in the community and in business was taking on the momentum of a roller coaster as I invested more time and energy in my achievements than in our relationship as a couple. The time I spent away from home left Eleanor as the sole support for our family instead of both of us sharing that load. During this time, we had plenty of arguments. Sometimes it seemed to be an exploding shell game; we were left wondering what would trigger the next conflict.

Eleanor had given up her dream medical job when we got married and was committed to staying home to raise the kids. Once they were all in school, I believe Eleanor yearned to work outside our home again, but now the opportunities were rare. And besides, from my perspective, why would she want to do that? Was I not a good provider? We had no need for a second income to provide for our family. But for her, there was something missing; she longed to experience herself as being more than a family caregiver. Though it seemed that too much time and space separated us as a couple, Eleanor continued to choose to stay home to be there for the family every step of the way.

In retrospect, I've realized that the priorities of family and relationships outweigh the need to have the world at our fingertips. I also came to understand the sacrifice Eleanor had made to marry me and support my endeavours, all at a huge personal cost to her. Sometimes I wished I could take back and do things over, but that was not to be.

Eleanor was a picture of health and vigour. Then, in the winter of 1986/87, she began experiencing fatigue and abdominal pain. We were soon caught up with the challenges of her emerging yet undiagnosed illness. In time, the problem was narrowed down to a possible gall bladder issue that could be dealt with later.

Due to the ongoing health issues Eleanor was facing, it was recommended that we go on a vacation, as on our return she would require surgery to remove her gall bladder. Wanting to take more time together as a family, we decided to go to California and take a West Coast tour through Los Angeles and down to San Diego. The vacation was all we imagined and hoped for, even though Eleanor struggled with pain, fatigue and the uncertainty of what lay ahead. We travelled through towns along the coastline, one of them being Delmar. The moment we saw the name, we recognized the acrostic: its letters were the initials of our family members' first names—Darryl, Eleanor, Lyndell, Martin and Rhonda. Delmar! We had a good laugh and suggested that, someday, we might have a company by that name!

Arriving back home, we expected life would carry on as usual; Eleanor would have the gallbladder surgery and nothing would change. The surgery date was in mid-June 1987, and all went well. She came home to recover, but things didn't seem quite right. Her condition continued to deteriorate so we went back to the doctor. They tried everything they knew of, but it offered no relief. Several weeks after surgery, she was rushed to the Health Sciences Centre in Winnipeg with doctors trying everything to find answers. While there, her temperature spiked and "went through the roof," and she was referred to a specialist, but the specialists, too, were at a loss to bring her fever down. Nothing worked. Finally, they resorted to placing her into a tub of ice water to reduce her body temperature, after which they reached a diagnosis. Eleanor had the dreaded disease called lupus. Without a known cure, this was a death sentence. It meant our lives would change.

Church, community and family rallied together to pray and support us as a family. As a couple, our lives were drawn together and we made a renewed effort in our marriage. On August 4, 1987, our nineteenth anniversary date, Eleanor was finally discharged from the Health Sciences Centre to return home. My life changed; I could see that her needs were much greater and more important than my ambitions.

I rented a Lincoln Town Car from Mr. Derksen at Hometown Ford to pick her up from the hospital. I had requested of Deb Kauenhoffen for CFAM radio to play Joey Gregorash's song "Together (The New Wedding Song)" as we headed for home. The timing was impeccable. I was driving down Ness Avenue in the West End of Winnipeg when the song came on; Eleanor was lying down in the back seat. I realized in that moment that the things I had taken for granted in life were truly the most important and needed to be cherished. All my accomplishments and service in the church meant nothing if my relationship with Eleanor was being neglected. We made a new commitment and stepped forward into the future, for a lifetime.

Life at home was changing forever. Dealing with terminal illness makes a family think, "How do we do this?" Many times, during a lupus flare-up, it didn't matter what had been planned ahead of time—schedules were readjusted, appointments missed, visits cut short, or else Eleanor just absorbed the pain and we carried on.

Eleanor was never one to complain in public and she never felt "sorry" for herself. She demonstrated a strong willpower to "suck it up," internalize what she was feeling and carry on. At times, that was hard to understand because it was only in the privacy of our home that her repressed emotional and physical pain showed up. She struggled with why God, why me and why now? Just as the opportunity was opening for her to step out into the workforce and interact with people, now it would be snatched away. Why would God not simply heal her as others were being healed? And why, indeed, would well-meaning people come to see us and accuse us of not having enough faith? Why, why, why?

Eleanor was an amazing woman who drew on strength that was only available because of her faith in God. It took a lot more faith to trust and believe in a God who cares when the darkness of doubt surrounded her than if instant healing had taken place. God would prove that in the next twenty-seven years of her life. Her community Bible study group, her church ladies' group and her extended family all rallied around to support our family. While we were occupied dealing with hospitals and doctors, thoughtful neighbours took our youngest daughter, Rhonda, on vacation with their family.

All the while, we dug deep into God's word, where Eleanor's scriptural strength was Philippians 4:13 (NKJV), "I can do all things through Christ who strengthens me." She held on to that verse every time she faced a challenge or when the pain seemed unbearable. Literally hundreds and hundreds of appointments with specialists and doctors would become the norm in the next few decades of dealing with the disease. Figuring out how to survive in a marriage and beyond, weathering this storm, enjoying life to the fullest, would be the challenge. Once more, my employer, Cargill, was very understanding and allowed me the time to take Eleanor to doctor appointments in Winnipeg.

Having health coverage that paid for the hundreds of thousands of dollars in medication bills not covered through Pharmacare was a blessing beyond words.

Trips to Winnipeg now turned into "date nights" or outings we could do together. Dinners and lunches out would become a part of every trip, celebrating another successful specialist visit. We took other opportunities to make the best of life as it was dealt to us. People and friends from near and far—prayer warriors—were praying that Eleanor's life would be prolonged till her children were adults. Elaine Giesbrecht, a valued friend of the family, prayed earnestly on Eleanor's behalf, "Lord, let me watch my children grow to see what they become." When I remember God's faithfulness to us, that song released by Mo Bandy in 1987, "Till I'm Too Old to Die Young," still brings tears to my eyes.

Very sadly, a few years later, Elaine herself passed away suddenly and never saw her own children grow up. The day Eleanor lost this dear friend and prayer supporter was a very hard day for her indeed. It was difficult for all of us to understand why God would spare Eleanor with her extreme suffering and take away her beautiful friend. As a family, we would try to return to normal, whatever that meant for us.

* * *

In 1991, my mother left this world for her eternal home. This hard working, very caring person meant the world to me. On Mother's Day, just before she passed away, I was driving past MacGregor where Mom and Dad lived, thinking how I would just love to take her for a walk in her wheelchair, just the two of us. She had some heart issues and struggled with dementia; my dad would always correct her memory lapses and it bothered her, which upset me. I just needed some one-on-one time with her. Life being busy, and it being late in the day, I did not stop by. I've regretted this frequently as I never had that chance again—she passed away the next week.

I have learned the lesson that, when I am prompted and convicted to do something, I should not put it off. I may never have another opportunity.

THIRTEEN:
Stepping Out into the Big League

Life in Winkler continued on the fast track. Being the Harvest Festival director during the years 1986 to 1989 and again in 1992 to 1993 was very rewarding, and huge crowds came to Winkler to celebrate. Once again, the time came for an offer to move to Elm Creek to be the director of operations there. Now, as in previous times but with more conviction than ever, I was determined not to move my family. Darryl and Lyn were in high school and Rhonda, a Mommy's girl in Grade 4, would not appreciate a move. Negotiations began, and I knew the third strike would be out if I could not make this work. I convinced them that I would accept the job in Elm Creek if Cargill would provide a new company car and pay for my travels to Elm Creek and back every day. This meant I could continue to carry out my volunteer responsibilities plus keep my job and take on a new challenge. Travel seemed tedious at times, but the job would prepare me for a future chapter of my life.

The year 1988 would prove to be very challenging. I had gone to Elm Creek for a week in December 1987 to get my bearings in the new job only to find the farm supply manager sitting in his office with his feet on the desk—not good. Then I went outside and found the current director of operations working on a piece of fertilizer equipment. Now, that was *not* a great way to start the day! I could tell why I needed to be there because that was *not* how I operated.

In January 1988, I began my new role in Elm Creek. There was a lot of pressure to rescue a sinking ship and turn the salvage into a profitable centre. I convinced the company that I wanted to make a few employee changes right out of the gate. The current marketing coordinator needed to leave, and I wanted a young fellow by the name of Jeff Johnston to replace him as my right-hand man. The rest of the staff was fairly accommodating, except for one member of the crew with whom things started off a bit rocky.

As I came in to work for real that January, I dressed up in a suit and tie, which I normally didn't do unless I was going to head office for a meeting. I closed the door to my farm supply manager's office and informed him that he'd had his last time sitting in his office with his feet on the desk and he would never see me fixing his equipment. It was not an easy start, but I continued to wear the suit and tie for a number of weeks to reinforce my statement. When the employee I didn't trust was transferred to Winnipeg, I was delighted that I didn't need to deal with him any longer, but the cleanup job would prove to be a bigger challenge.

Elm Creek was Cargill's flagship, their first inland terminal and only one hour from head office in Winnipeg, so there were many visitors. This was also the only location that was able to manage its own grain futures accounts, which meant we were able to "play" the markets. It's interesting that, at the time, teletype services were being used to communicate grain purchases, but we didn't own a computer or a fax machine!

A Scrappy Little Nobody

For me, this was a new chapter for sure, and I would tackle this in the same way I had tackled difficult situations before: I had a task, I would work hard and we would work together as a team to make this facility the flagship it was designed to be.

Little did I realize that seven years of tenure in Elm Creek (1988 to 1995) would give me a "master's education" in psychology, computer science, technology and marketing, and a rating as designated market maker in the Winnipeg Stock Exchange, all in the same course!

My levels of training increased along with my responsibilities, and as time went on, it seemed I was not only having a major impact on the farming community around Elm Creek but also in the larger market share from outside the region. Farmers from 150 miles away hauled in grain. We provided farm pick-up options by hiring local truckers as well as a single truck owned by Cargill and operated by a local driver. The base was already somewhat established when I brought in another dynamic from the Hutterite customers with whom I'd started doing business as a salesman at Clark's Poultry Farm and Hatchery some eighteen years earlier. When the "Big Three" arrived from Aspenheim Colony at Bagot, they came straight to my office and business got done. The Big Three were brothers and included Jake, the secretary; Levi, the farm manager; and Rueben, the minister. All three were three hundred pounds plus, so needless to say, their presence was noticed.

The employee I didn't trust, for good reason, left quite the mess, which took some time to sort out. Fake contracts were plentiful. He had used those to put on futures positions that would not easily be traced. The acceptable way to contract grain was through a phone call or a handshake, rarely backed up by a signed contract. That might not have been an issue under normal market conditions; however, when the markets became volatile, you could be caught on the wrong side faster than the blink of an eye. So, when the truth came out, we found literally hundreds of unsigned contracts; most were legit, but too many were not. We painstakingly verified which were authentic and which needed to be cancelled, and discovered that we were left with a significant loss on the books. However, that was when things became interesting. The legitimate contracts needed follow-up to ensure deliveries were made to cover the obligation.

The summer of 1988 came and with it a huge drought, sending the markets skyrocketing. Integrity became an issue and money became the driving factor in the pursuit of success. Choices had to be made: to deal with honesty or give in to inertia and slide down a slippery slope to negate the obligations previously made.

I had developed a good rapport with the Hutterite colonies. They were familiar with my beliefs, and since their fundamental faith was similar, we had a clear understanding. On one occasion, I was dealing with a colony close to Portage la Prairie when honesty and integrity came to the test. I spoke initially with the farm manager, who had a contract commitment to deliver canola at a fixed price. He claimed he had not signed the contract; therefore, he was not obligated to deliver the grain and could take it somewhere else for more money. When it seemed that talking to him would be futile, I decided it would be appropriate to chat with the minister and find out where he stood on the issue. The colony minister carries the final word and has a lot of power. I made the call and explained the situation and the agreement. We chatted generally about our word being as good as a signature; then I asked if their concept of our word being reliable was not considered important. The next day, the trucks began rolling in and the deliveries were made to fulfill their responsibility. The strength of that relationship had been over a decade in the making. Difficult times reveal who is trustworthy and who would walk for a few dollars.

Dealing with over a hundred different colonies was a challenge; however, once a good relationship was intact, Hutterites were the most generous and loving people around. Years before, I had established guidelines: I would never bribe them with alcohol or freebees because that business was normally short-lived. When the gifts stopped, so did the business. The best approach was to get to know them, be a real friend and maintain the business because we were reliable and would treat them with respect. I must say, that established the framework of our business interactions and lasted a lifetime!

As we concluded some very difficult situations with contracts, the next problem to address was the drought and the poor crops produced that resulted in a severe shortage of feed grains and oilseeds.

Since the Elm Creek location was equipped with underused grain cleaners, we made the decision not to ship out any uncleaned feed grain. Instead, we would clean every bushel we took in. Before long, we had a great market established with a successful businessman, Morris Rodin, widely and congenially known as "The Rat," who owned Central Grain on Archibald Street in Winnipeg. Central Grain pelletized the screenings, converting them into good quality cattle feed. It didn't take long before that market was as high as feed barley, and screenings were being shipped back west from the terminal in Thunder Bay, Ontario, to help supply feed stock for livestock in Manitoba.

It was at that time that I decided it would be a powerful marketing tool to start paying our farm customers for the screenings, which were normally worthless. That was a hard sell, convincing the grain traders and my boss in Winnipeg that we should do that. Well, we did and made good money in that market! The practice was soon followed by other smaller grain firms, but the "big boys" or central driven grain companies didn't seem to be able to catch the wave of opportunity we had developed. This proved the value of independent thinkers' ability to make incredible marketing decisions that would mean the difference between losing money and making money. We drew the attention of the corporate Cargill structure. Interest in what we were doing spread, and other locations with cleaning capacity joined in to create more opportunities.

We had many foreign dignitaries from Cargill's head office in Winnipeg show up to tour our facility. On one memorable occasion, it was a Chinese delegation. As was the norm, every delegate came equipped with a high-end camera and this time was no exception. We had excellent staff at Elm Creek; however, one stood out above everyone else: Big Pete Terwin. Pete was the plant equipment operator, and he unloaded a lot of the trucks. He was a very jovial man. Pete stepped out from operating the cleaners into the elevator driveway—his size quite the contrast to the less-than-five-feet-tall Chinese guys—lifted his hands above his head and yelled out, "KING KONG!" I doubt there was a single delegate not familiar with the *King Kong* movie—there was instant recognition! Everyone wanted their picture taken with this guy who (according to their standards) was a giant. I don't believe they had another question for me because Pete had stolen the show! No doubt he also became the showstopper when the delegation returned to China with photos of our facility.

The following fiscal year (June 1, 1988 to May 31, 1989) turned out to be the year where Cargill in Elm Creek handled the least amount of grain on record—not quite why I was transferred there—but produced the best bottom line they had experienced for some time! I learned, then and there, that better management meant better returns and that volume, if not handled correctly, did not produce the best results.

As the business continued to expand, so did the opportunities. Volumes improved, and we became more heavily involved in the farm supply business. We purchased an off-site farm supply facility complete with a dry fertilizer storage shed and an anhydrous ammonia business. We expanded to add liquid fertilizer services as well as agronomy services. That led to the addition of a custom fertilizer and chemical application business, and before we realized it, we were operating a $3-million farm service business out of that location—one of the highest in the country.

Marketing this business and financing it was a challenge, especially when the individual farm cash flow was tight. I developed a plan that would further enhance the business. We offered deferred billing of chemicals and fertilizer till fall, tying it into enhanced grain deliveries. It was called the LIFT program, short for "lower interest financing terms." It was a hit and obviously attracted more, but also riskier, customers. Careful management of that program would be critical, and it was speculative. But it proved to be the right decision. Some customers couldn't pay in full the same year and struggled to find alternate financing, so obviously I had some pushback. Eventually bills got paid, and we gained more established and very loyal customers. That also helped farmers recognize that we understood them, and as long as we could get the job done together, it was good for all. Instead of handling 68,000 tonnes of grain like we did in 1988/89, the business boomed to over 120,000 to 130,000 tonnes on a consistent basis.

* * *

I had it down pat: it was fifty-five minutes to the dot travelling to work and back home. It also meant leaving home in the dark and returning in the dark most days, especially if overtime was involved or when meetings took place in Winnipeg. Our once idyllic country living, with two kids in high school who worked after school to earn a few bucks, had become a bit of a burden by 1992. So, we started looking for Winkler properties of similar value with more conveniences. To make life simpler, we decided to purchase a "spec home" on Southview Drive in Winkler from a local builder. This would shorten the drive by ten minutes and offer other in-town opportunities.

Considering Eleanor's struggle with illness, home life continued to be a challenge. Cargill understood that my home was important to me and that my wife would need to make many trips into Winnipeg to see specialists. They allowed me the flexibility to take extra time to look after the home-front needs. Since I was paid a monthly salary, the paycheque never varied; the job got done and the results were positive.

One wintry morning at 5:00 a.m., with the temperature at minus 35 degrees Celsius, unable to sleep, I set out to work. Before I left Winkler, I stopped at the Royal Bank of Canada (RBC), leaving the car running to keep it warm as I made a deposit. Going back to the car, I found out the doors had locked! There were no cell phones at the time, so with my car still running, I walked the three full blocks to a twenty-four-hour drive-thru service at Tempo Hi-Way. Inappropriately dressed as I was for the bitterly freezing temperatures, I stopped at their window and reluctantly asked to borrow their phone. It may have been my imagination, but it seemed to me it got a little chillier when my good wife answered the phone, crawled out from under the warm covers, bundled up and—wide awake now—climbed into a second car to bring me an extra set of keys.

***

Since a good chunk of my business was done with Hutterite colonies, I became acutely aware of both sides of a "religious" dispute going on inside the colonies. The split in opinion came to be known as the "Gibbers" and the "Oilers," with the bishop of the colonies getting involved in outside investments in Texas oil wells and New York manufacturing. The story became public knowledge when Don Gibb wrote a book about Hutterite issues and the conflict, implicating the top bishop of misappropriating church funds, thereby drawing a line in the sand. The conservative "Gibbers" were very opposed to putting additional money in New York investments or Texas oil wells, especially when the oil wells produced no oil! The issue was exacerbated with the infusion of money into Spring Hill Farms hog slaughtering plant at Neepawa. Money was flowing out faster than hot water through a sieve, and tempers flared. Efforts were being made to automatically deduct a portion of the cheques and put it into the church funds, to the point of attempting to create a credit card for all purchases where a percentage would go to the church.

Religion aside, this had to be stopped. Having customers on both sides of the split meant this would need to be handled very delicately or I would lose both. With that in mind, I offered our board room at Elm Creek as a neutral zone. They did meet in private, but nothing was resolved. That was not the end, however, as a farm boss at one of the colonies was determined to take out his family share and leave the conservative colony where he was a member. That did not end well, as we received grain "in trust" pending a court decision as to the ownership of the grain. In a way, it seemed okay as both sides trusted me to be neutral, and that was only accomplished because of the years I'd spent establishing trusting, impartial relationships.

I continued to do business with both sides, but grain deliveries had to be staggered to avoid driveway brawls! The saddest part was the internal splitting, with family pitted against family and children who couldn't return to their parents even to observe a funeral. Some colonies actually had security guards in place to ensure the offenders never set foot on their adversaries' property! This was certainly a sad time, and I needed to tread softly on all fronts so I did not get caught up in the fray. Those days saw the greatest shift in how colonies would do business and how they would literally survive the conflict.

There was a positive pathway out of this adversity. In the foray of relationships splintering, colony members not only became acutely aware of their relationships with each other but also their relationship with God, and who and what they represented. They began to understand they were actually not an island unto themselves and became keenly aware of their surroundings and the needs of this world. They were no longer reluctant to donate money for good causes, including the medical and mental health services offered by "outside" organizations. I can only hope that I was one of the positive influencers to that end, as my association with the colonies and affection for them continued to be valued even to the present time.

FOURTEEN:
Managing Business and People

The challenges at Elm Creek continued, from trying to find savings in operational costs to having the right staff in place to continue growing the business. The first thing I learned was that the old MTS phone modem had been in place for twelve years, and we were paying $110 per month to rent it! After enquiring with MTS, I discovered the modem had been fully redeemed for years. Checking at the electronics store, I found we could buy a brand new one for less than a month's rent on the old one! Obviously, this was a small thing, but if you don't address the small things, you will miss the big ones. The old adage "a penny saved is a penny earned" was where I came from.

Change meant some hard decisions would need to be made, including for some of the office staff. In those days, smoking in offices was a normal, acceptable practice and true in Elm Creek as well. We had eight people working in the office, two of them were the grain accounting and farm supply accounting clerks. I struggled for months with breathing and allergy concerns where I would literally sneeze all day and go home stuffed up and exhausted. Sitting next to my office in an open area, without fail, the two accounting girls never extinguished their cigarettes, allowing the nicotine-laced fumes to smoulder in the ash tray till it was time to light the next one. Remember, back in my youth, how I was tempted to smoke like the rest of the kids and be popular? Well, I believe that lesson was a gift and God gave me an allergy to smoke as a reminder. I addressed this issue with the staff involved and was promptly told it was their right to smoke in the office, and no, they would not compromise by waiting till coffee break in order to contain the tobacco smoke to one room. One day, I'd had enough. I informed them how things would be in the future and that they could no longer smoke at their desks. The company didn't have such a policy, but I could not do my job properly under the current conditions. Things got "a bit tense" between us, and the two employees threatened to walk out and quit. Well, I don't appreciate threats, and I was not about to be held hostage by them. I called their bluff, thinking they would not be stupid enough to give up a great job for the privilege of smoking. As they repeated their previous attempt to intimidate me, I simply said, "I have come here to do a job and I am not leaving; I can't stay this way, so you decide what you're going to do." They walked, and we were left scrambling to do the work.

I brought back a former employee on a temporary basis, and wow, did that ever change the atmosphere in the office! It brought unity in purpose, a welcome atmosphere of comradery and a new day for my personal health as well as the health of visitors who came to the office. The work was getting done and no one missed a beat. I am convinced that none of us are irreplaceable regardless of how important we may feel. This was the beginning of changes in corporate policy where smoking was banned in every Cargill facility across Canada. I was just about six months ahead of the curve or, should I say, the trailblazer of things to come. After that, new government regulations were set in place changing the smoking rules for the nation.

The controversy and animosity between the Canadian Wheat Board (CWB) and the open market raged. There were hard lines on both sides, and I am sure I saw only a small segment. We had an elected CWB representative named Butch Harder from Lowe Farm. Although he and I originated from the same region and carried the same name, we were on opposite sides of the issue. At public meetings, where he often spoke and gave updates on the "pool" accounts held by the board, I was not afraid to challenge him. The farming community clearly understood that having the same name did not mean having the same perspective. I had corporate support for my comments, as I gave a fair and positive picture of different marketing alternatives. My philosophy was more in the field of flexibility and timing in marketing, allowing those needing to market grain to do so when they chose, in place of a permit system that allowed deliveries only when the CWB needed the grain. As if the farmer was not smart enough to make his own decisions! At least that was how I looked at it. Every time I loaded a railcar for export, I saw a job being shipped out to another country. I could just imagine how productive this country could be if we processed our own grain and created jobs to do that in Canada.

I saw the canola market develop and then looked at the malt barley business, restricted to a few plants that had to buy their product from the board. I saw the lack of flour mills in Canada and how the entire Durham wheat crop was shipped to Europe with no Canadian processing. It was during this time that the federal government changed to a Conservative government. A great friend and customer back in my Sidney days, Charlie Mayer became the federal minister in charge of the CWB. The rumours started about how this government would dismantle the CWB, taking sole control of Western Canadian wheat, oats and barley from the CWB.

Cracks began to form; however, resistance was so great that on the first go-around only oats were removed. The market for oats was a losing proposition, used by the CWB as an "also ran" in their marketing approach. Growing oats was a last resort when you couldn't grow anything else. The CWB had been established during the Second World War to accommodate the sale of grain products into England. However, it only applied to Western Canada. My question was why did it still exist and for what purpose? And if it was the *Canadian* Wheat Board, why was Eastern Canada not included? Why were the majority of flour mills in Eastern Canada? And why were flour mills developed into a very large enterprise in the United States?

So, why was there such an uproar when Charlie Mayer introduced the removal of oats from the CWB control? Over ten years before, back in 1974 to 1976, changes made to the CWB's powers (removing their exclusive marketing rights regarding the private sale of feed grains for animals within Western Canada) had made the cattle feed industry boom. I felt that now the writing was on the wall and prepared for the total abolition of the board. In 1989, Charlie Mayer removed oats from CWB control in record time; August 1 was the beginning of the new crop year, and it was done! This opened the doors of imagination to where we could go. The change was a springboard to oats becoming a valued health crop. Construction began for the development of many oat-processing plants in Manitoba and Western Canada.

Since the ultimate end of the CWB on August 1, 2012, processing grain into edible food products has become the norm in Canada. Literally thousands of new jobs reduced our dependency on food imports, creating a robust economy right here at home. It remains ironic how the naysayers still insist it was an "economic tragedy," as it was termed by former National Farmers Union (NFU) president Terry Boehm in a 2020 hindsight article reflecting the NFU's perspective.[1] Former Minister Gerry Ritz is painted as swinging the wrecking ball in 2012, ending once and for all the CWB monopoly in Canada. Those who are gainfully employed in Canada and those farmers who have seen tremendous opportunities to diversify their farms would surely have to disagree. I dare say that the CWB would have self-imploded because farmers have and will continue to grow marketable crops that show the best returns to support their operation. Customer service still prevails as the best way to ensure the business remains supported and viable in an ever-changing environment. In my opinion, the CWB had lost their way; it had become more self-protectionist and less focused on supporting farmers, and that's why they needed to be removed. This change brought endless opportunities for many for which we are all better off today.

But it wasn't a smooth process. By the mid-nineties, revolutionary farmers began to revolt, saying, "Enough is enough," and crossed the U.S. border to deliver their own grain into higher market-driven values. Independent grain marketers got involved and shipped grain across the border without CWB consent or permits. Tickets were issued that really didn't come close to preventing this exodus of Manitoba farmers with their wheat.

Eventually the CWB brought a halt to this procedure, at the expense of every free market thinker around. It actually smelled like a controlled society, almost Soviet Union style.

---

[1] Terry Boehm, "2020 hindsight: Ending the Canadian wheat board was an economic tragedy," National Farmers Union website, July 30, 2020, https://www.nfu.ca/2020-hindsight-ending-the-canadian-wheat-board-was-an-economic-tragedy.

How can it be wrong to simply sell your own grown goods? To this very day, that debate continues in the quota system of market regulation.

Bringing the focus back to Elm Creek in the early nineties, we had our own pressing issue: the devastating effects of mould. In the year 1992/93, fusarium mould attacked cereal grain production hard. It was a harrowing year, and the government agricultural insurance organization encouraged farmers to dig a hole and bury the crop or simply burn it in the field. Even grain companies, including Cargill, were hesitant to handle it or take it into the elevator. With huge oat contracts on the books and farmers wanting to deliver, we were told not to take it into the facility. We decided to place the deliveries into designated bins, but we did take it in.

By apparently "working against the grain," I found the dire years of 1992 to 1994 became the best years for me at Cargill. I had a reputation of not liking to stick to the "box" and being willing to try different things. We realized the amount of protein in this disease-infected crop was going through the roof! At the same time, it was very apparent that U.S. winter wheat, as well as spring wheat, was very low in protein, so flour mills, mostly in the United States, were starving for protein. We could do a fairly decent job of cleaning the grain, removing a lot of the visibly infected kernels as they were basically empty and selling a decent, good-looking sample. Since this product was feed-grain quality, we could purchase the grain as non-CWB, then take out a feed permit from the board, mix it with CWB wheat and ship it to U.S. mills.

ConAgra Foods had a flour mill in the Minneapolis area, which made access pretty convenient by truck. We tried a few loads and they loved it! It brought their protein up nicely and became an excellent bread wheat. We continued that out of Elm Creek, where I was buying wheat destined for the garbage at one dollar per bushel on the free market and selling it as milling wheat to U.S. millers. I convinced Robin Hood in Saskatoon to try some, but since they were unionized, they could not take in any wheat that was diseased. Finally, we did send them two loads during the night shift. They tried it and it was great; however, politics prevented that market from expanding.

Since we were the Cargill guinea pigs on this project, the margins we were making was not lost on Cargill management. Some independent companies were also starting to get into the act, buying the product for fifty to seventy-five cents per bushel; the farmers would simply collect on the crop insurance to cover the rest. I was under pressure to reduce my bid, but I felt we were well rewarded and that it simply would not be necessary to gouge profits from producers. The argument was put to rest and we continued. In fact, the U.S. Cargill flour mills cut in when they discovered we were shipping it to ConAgra and it was working well. Soon Cargill decided all our wheat was to be shipped to its flour mills, adding other Cargill locations into this program.

This was great for me, as the Cargill bonus system was based on profitability and I could earn up to 50 percent of my salary in bonuses. My goal was not for personal gain, as I had reached the 50 percent of my salary mark early in the year. My goal now was to see how far we could go and what records we could set. I was very aware that it was much more than management who was responsible for achieving these levels. Other members of our staff were equally important in the success of these endeavours. Not only was the paperwork more intense now, the service performed by the cleaning staff was exceptional and I wanted them to be included in the bonus distribution. To this day, it saddens me that these team players were not rewarded. It began to take its toll in a loss of my respect for this great organization. The margins were tremendous, but after being distributed to other departments in head office marketing, the portion of profits distributed to our Elm Creek location was limited. That was hard to accept, even though we ended up with the highest bottom line in the history of Elm Creek. The next few years would be tough to handle, as my business philosophy and Cargill's ideology were on the cusp of a major divergence.

FIFTEEN:
Midlife Crisis and the Exodus

I was working on a massive computer program to incorporate all operations and combine them into one comprehensive computer program. I felt unqualified, but that was the piece I liked about this company. They trusted me with more than I could ever imagine. Having been in the Minneapolis office a number of times to work on this project, it seemed normal and right to be involved. From an operational perspective, I was there to review the work that programmers had put together for our use—it was fun! The meeting room in Minneapolis was on the same floor as the meeting room where we met in Winnipeg, and both were close to the lunch room. So, when I received an invitation indicating exactly where in the building this meeting was to be held, I drove to Winnipeg. No one was in the room. That was strange, so I called the coordinator, who informed me the meeting was in Minneapolis! Needless to say, I missed that one and realized that it's always best to carefully read the whole invitation.

For me, 1994/95 became a year of decision. Cargill was once a company where I could make decisions that I felt were best; suddenly, it seemed the pressure was on to conform to

Cargill policy—and I am not quite a policy-type person. If I have an idea that makes sense and is legal, why is there a procedure that discourages it? There was a program in place where we could apply to get funds for a project that had a five-year return on investment (ROI); it made sense, but it was about to change. Real-time discussions were taking place about our futures. At the end of the discussions, would we even be in the farm supply business? I had no idea what was being discussed behind the scenes, but what was being talked about around the water cooler did not sit well with me. I did have projects that fit the three-year ROI, and I was fortunate enough to get some approved, but not many. I had just come through the 1994 fiscal year end on May 31. I saw numbers that were absolutely astounding and I knew we were a big part of that success, so why was I displeased and dissatisfied? I had never made as much money in my life, but the fundamental shift in the company had left me lacking purpose and feeling unappreciated.

In the fall, I began musing about my concerns with my boss at the time, Bruce Sobkow, the vice-president. These changes and the absence of management's consideration when failing to share the bonus with other employees bothered me; I even discussed taking some of my bonus and redistributing it to my co-workers. The answer was a solid "No," which left me confused and disappointed.

There was one perk: I was invited on a tour of Lake Minnetonka where many of Cargill world corporate executives have their mansions. I had been there for training and for working on projects a number of times, but this was different. It was an extraordinary event—it certainly should have been an honour to be on this private yacht, meeting the world president of Cargill. After all, he was there to say thanks for a great performance. Even so, and even there, I simply lacked the ability to get with the program and to feel genuinely acknowledged.

Conversations continued on a regular basis about what I felt could change. The assumption was that I was unhappy at Elm Creek and needed a new challenge. I was invited to run a terminal in Calgary and I was offered a position as the fertilizer purchaser for all of Canada, but neither of these opportunities changed the corporate issue I was struggling with. It was still the same company; I sensed that my time at Cargill was winding down.

I tried to leave the idea until after Christmas and into the new year of 1995, but my thoughts continued to weigh heavily on my heart. I talked to Eleanor about it, as well as some family, who wondered if I had slipped a few marbles—leaving the best-paid job I ever had and thinking I could go on my own?! Financial management was pretty important to me, so I assured Eleanor I would not leave my job as long as I had any debt. Based on my employment history and the connections I had with my farming friends, including colonies, I would adjust our needs according to what I could generate as income. In January 1995, it all came together. I paid off my mortgage, bought an older car, and was footloose and debt free! All I needed to do financially was put food on the table and continue with my commitments to give ten percent to the Lord's work—a lesson learned well that has stuck through the years.

At the end of January, I met with my boss one more time to discuss the reasons behind why I had said no to several opportunities. I had made my decision and was giving one month's notice of my departure. I informed him that I was embarking on a different path for myself, the "grain brokerage" business, which would be in the same category as the ones I used to call the "rinke-dinks." I was fully expecting to be asked to clean out my desk, park my company car and call Eleanor to come pick me up. That would have been the normal corporate protocol for someone in my position. What happened next shocked me and also reminded me that burning bridges only hurts the ones with the match.

My boss said, "Martin, you know this business like the back of your hand. You have a great reputation and I am not concerned that you will take anything of value. You have your customer list in your head. The decision about when you leave, that's entirely up to you. You will know over the next month when that time is. If you find the customers coming in are here to talk only about your future endeavours, that will be the time you call me and that can be your exit."

Conversation done; very generous indeed! On the other hand, our pension plan was really not that good and after twenty-one years in their employ, all I had was an accumulated $50,000 value designed to pay off after forty years! I worked for another three weeks when it happened, and I made the call that I was done. Then I called my wife; she came to pick me up and I was on my own! The final bonus came when I opened up my last paycheque: they had added an additional $10,000 to my pension RRSP.

Having been given the opportunity to operate as if I owned the business, I had grown as an independent thinker. In fact, those were my instructions: "Martin, treat this as if you were on your own." So, I was well prepared to live with the consequences of my mistakes and the benefits of good decisions. I was embarking on a journey into the world of free enterprise, and that would serve me well in the next chapter of my life. Yes, it was scary to a point—no one else, including my wife, thought this was a great idea. I was on my own. In spite of her misgivings, Eleanor backed me and encouraged me, but inside, I believe she was terrified. In my mind, I had this figured out. My skills were managing, selling and building relationships. These attributes were about to become even more valuable in the next chapter of my life.

Before I reached the summer of 1995, I came to believe the reason I was treated so well was because my departure (as I liked to term it) was the beginning of a significant exodus of Cargill's major players. My former boss, Bruce Sobkow, and his boss (also formerly my boss), Curt Vossen, the president of Cargill, left to become the president and vice-president of Pioneer Grain in the Richardson family of companies. Over the course of that year, many people left Cargill to take on other challenges in their respective lives. I had no way of knowing if I had planted the first seeds of change or if those seeds were already fully germinated when I left. Given the generous way in which I was treated, was I the benefactor or the beneficiary of a bumper crop? While my own good times with Cargill ended with this stage, it was onward and upward.

My first purchase—the Jordan Pool Elevator, September 1996

Midlife Crisis and the Exodus

My father at eighty-seven years old, in amazement at his son owning an elevator

SIXTEEN:
More than a Rinke-Dink

Over the year 1995, I closed old files and turned the page to a new chapter in my life. I had been involved as a partner in a local truck repair shop some years earlier, and when it disbanded, we were left with a corporation without any activity. After a year of paying returns for an inactive company, I asked my partners if I could "buy" their shares and keep filing returns until a useful opportunity came up. This was the time for our dream of owning a corporation called Delmar to become a reality! I simply applied for a name change of an existing partnership, and there we were! The shares were fifty-five for me and forty-five for Eleanor. The registered name became Delmar Commodities Ltd.

At forty-six years of age, and for the first time since 1970, I would not be guaranteed a paycheque. Getting to the debt-free zone meant everything. Selling our home on Southview Drive and purchasing an older home on Aspen Bay made it possible to move forward and achieve new successes. Our daughter Lyn was now married and had moved to Regina, but Darryl and Rhonda were still at home; Darryl worked at Co-op Gas Bar as the manager and Rhonda was in high school. I received a lot of advice about how I should start the business from home and save money, but that didn't appeal to me. I felt there needed to be a "home refuge" similar to the separation I required between church and business. I felt church shouldn't be the place to gain business contacts and a home-based business wouldn't have the opportunity to grow into what I had imagined. I ended up renting a location on Main Street in Winkler, where I set up an office.

I was very aware of my own interpretation of grain brokers as "Rinke-dinks," but I was willing to swallow my pride and give it a shot. Adjusting my lifestyle to fit my income meant I had to quickly set up a plan for how I could secure an income to look after our obligations and put food on the table. I set out to connect with my customers and friends, including a number of colonies and larger farmers. I offered to be their "grain marketing" agent for one dollar per acre farmed up to a maximum of $5,000 per farmer per year, regardless of size. It worked well and I had great contract agreements. The first year, I signed up enough farmers with faith in me to give them advice and find markets for their grain to generate almost $100,000 in income. As a further service, companies who needed grain could pay me fifty cents per tonne to deliver it to them.

A number of things happened that first year. I discovered who was honest and who was willing to short circuit the system—to sell or buy directly from the farm and not pay me at all! In any case, it was an easy transition. I didn't need cash to own the grain, and I was never liable for the quality of the grain because it went directly from the grower to the end user. The next challenge as the year progressed was the issue that some producers trusted me and so didn't want a cheque from the individual or company I was selling to. That began the slippery slope of paying for the grain through my company, Delmar Commodities Ltd. Since I was not a licensed grain company, I would need to face the scrutiny of the Canadian Grain Commission and their licensing department. This would become a difficult road as I also needed to be bonded, and acquiring a bond would not be easy without a history, besides being very expensive! My son, Darryl, empathized with me and offered to come work for me to help run the office. He was a tremendous asset, as he was organized, loved paperwork and inspired me. Together we realized a dream that was bigger than my own. We were a great team; I could teach him the skills needed to run a company and he could keep me organized.

The next year, 1996, brought additional challenges as my grain purchasing required an operating line of credit to carry the inventory and receivables. Two vital decisions needed to be made. The first was that I needed a reliable banker who understood the business and would support it in difficult times. My first banker had big plans to give me a $30,000 operating loan to function. Well, I thought that would work for one day, but what would I do the next? I would not be able to get into buying grain at all. As it happened, there was another banker who saw things differently. Fred Stock at RBC was my account manager, and he wanted to help me get going. Little did we know what this venture would become.

Later in the spring of 1996, a group of local board members from Jordan Pool Elevator came to see me about buying their elevator. It was fortunate for them that they never gave up their property ownership to the pool, which allowed them to negotiate a deal out of their handling agreement and sell the elevator. The problem for me was I had no money. I had negotiated an operating line that was barely enough to pay for the odd load of grain, never mind a full elevator. How do you buy an elevator and fill it with grain with no money?

Negotiations continued in earnest, with me not letting on what my fears were, but simply pretending I could pull this off. Perhaps the bank would come through or maybe there would be other means to finance this project. This was when we reached a final price of $150,000 for the facility, and I would take over August 1, 1996.

Our house was jointly owned and paid for, and I had promised my wife that I would never put her in jeopardy where we would need to move. Her health was too volatile to add stress to her life, so I tried to keep that promise in order.

I reached back into my friend list and remembered a great Hutterite friend I had made back in 1971 in the Clark's Poultry Farm days. I had serviced Riverbend Colony, close to Carberry. Our friendship was unconditional and the colony was prosperous, so why would I not approach them for an opportunity to partner in this venture? My standards of business investment through Cargill were very aggressive. I thought, if it worked there, perhaps I should use the same formula in this venture. The colony was not interested in partnership; however, when I presented Mike with the notion that I would pay them half of my profits for three years, his interest was piqued. He said he would talk to the colony and ask his accountant and lawyer for advice. I asked him for $175,000 to purchase the facility and to replace the old scale with one that could weigh semi-trailers. He called back a few weeks later.

"The advice I got," he said, "was to say 'No.'" I was deflated until he continued. "But since I know you, I will do it under one condition. If in three years, the principal amount has not been paid, you still owe us the principal, but I will not charge you any interest." How much better could this get?

I said, "Yes," and without even a handshake or written agreement, we met on Highway 1 beside the road at the Oakville corner, and he handed me a cheque for $175,000. I realized once again the importance of not burning bridges and maintaining friendships that hold their value if treated with respect.

In our grain brokerage business, we were very actively purchasing soymeal in the United States and supplying hog farms in Manitoba. Not having truck traffic going that direction, we ran out of options to bring the soymeal back, so we attempted to transport the meal in railcars. I arranged with the local pool board that, since we were taking possession of the elevator on August 1, I could use the rail spur at Jordan to unload. Common courtesy meant I would visit the elevator to inform the manager of the arrival of the cars and let him know that we would appreciate the use of the scales.

Walking into the elevator, I realized why this business was not successful. The manager was sitting in his office watching soap operas. He showed little ambition to help. He informed us when his golf games were scheduled and, according to union rules, when the doors closed. We would try to work around that; however, when the cars arrived in 30-degree-Celsius heat, the product had to be removed one chunk at a time, so unloading became cumbersome and time consuming. In the end, when the doors closed at 4:55 p.m., the rest of our trucks had to go to Miami, nine miles away, to weigh, empty and load. To be frank, that set the stage for how my company would be different. Delmar's customer service would mean something and people would be treated with respect.

The day came when possession was fully in my hands, the elevator was paid for, the scale construction was underway and business began in earnest. My son, Darryl, would manage the office; Ed Penner was hired to run the elevator; and I would buy the grain. I recall when the first load of grain was delivered, how it felt now that I owned the grain in that elevator! Honestly, it was a bit overwhelming, but as the business progressed, it became easier. If I were to ship by rail, I needed access to terminal unloading facilities in Thunder Bay and Vancouver. Cash flow would be tight as I became an official agent of the dreaded Canadian Wheat Board. Again, friendships and relationships came in handy as I reached an agreement with Pioneer Grain, where my former boss from Cargill ended up working. Having a ready market there helped with my cash flow, and Pioneer Grain also helped finance my CWB inventory.

The business was off to a great start. Profits were good and we enjoyed the challenges of growing the business. My accountant was Gislason Targownik Peters in Winkler and my banker, RBC. As I had learned back in my shoebox accounting days, these two professionals were still the cornerstone of any business venture. Attempts were made to dissuade me from running my own business. There were those who were certain I could never compete with the huge terminals, but I was bound and determined to prove them wrong. I was extremely flexible in my business; by the time the "Big Boys" figured out what I was up to, I could change direction and try something else before they caught up. It was fun, and I was growing into a formidable option in the grain market, soon not to be a Rinke-dink anymore!

After the second-year end, the principal obligation I had with Riverbend Colony was fully paid off, but I had one more year in the contract per my agreement. At the end of three years, they received double the amount they had invested. It was the highest interest I've ever paid in my life, but it was also the best investment I ever made. Certainly, a promise kept would be the best recipe for success. The saying, "A handshake is as good as a signed piece of paper," held true as the business continued to flourish. I may have been a small player, but I played an important role in the industry. It seemed like we were definitely the equalizer that provided options for local customers.

A Scrappy Little Nobody

Top 50 Manitoba Business Award recognition as the *Manitoba Business Magazine* fastest growing company

Delmar annual fishing trip to Eagle Nest Lodge on the Winnipeg River

SEVENTEEN:
A Booming Business

The Jordan corner had never seen so much activity. Customers were coming from a hundred miles away to do business with us. My company was not driven by great aspirations to become rich or reach a specific business target. My business plan was simple: look after the customers I have and they will look after the customers to come; together we build relationships going forward. We had a continuation of great connections with hog producers and colonies, providing them with grain and soybean meal for protein supplements. Darryl continued to keep the accounting straight, and as we established more support in the office, we hired staff to help manage the accounting load. When office space in the elevator became too dirty and crowded for all, we weighed the benefits of building additional office space attached to the elevator. It is likely that what tipped the balance in favour of separate office space was seeing Michelle Thiessen standing on her desk, screaming for the elevator manager to get rid of a mouse while, equally terrified, Ed Penner tried to catch the little varmint from a distance.

I always had a tough time putting together a "business plan" for an unknown future. This time, though I didn't know where my business was heading, I recognized it was not the accepted, normal way to grow a business. One thing I did know and held firm to was that if I served my customers well, word of mouth would be my best advertising. Once good relationships were established, my customers would likely be understanding and help me out in a crunch.

I was never one to appreciate "overhead" employees, so my conversation with Darryl went like this: "You manage the soymeal sales and delivery side. Your objective is to earn enough revenue to pay for your accounting work to be free and not a burden to our bottom line. I will stick to the grain marketing side and overall management of the company." I guess it was a somewhat diversified management approach and employee training in the same basket.

My dad was eighty-seven years old when he stopped by the elevator one day. Looking at the facility and the trucks lined up, he asked me, "Son, how will you ever pay for this?" To him it was a daunting business proposition and seemed impossible, but I was very optimistic about our success and somewhat bold in my approach. I regret that Dad passed away in the spring of 1998 without seeing the success this business became.

Another "wise" industry associate's rather negative response to me starting a company and being successful was "Martin, you are this company and it will never be anything once you are not here." Now if you ever wanted to get me fired up, that type of comment would do it!

I knew I needed more help. I remembered two people I had worked with or watched in the industry who I thought could be added to create a strong, solid team. Both individuals were working for Pioneer Grain, the same company where my former Cargill boss was employed. How could I convince them to make the same move I'd made? I started with what I thought was the biggest need: someone to be in charge of the operating side. I had hired a young gentleman back in the Sidney days, a very down-to-earth, dependable employee who became a good friend. He left Cargill before I did and was employed at Pioneer Grain, successfully running a brand-new facility at Mollard. How would I convince him that this company could provide a brighter future for him than working all his life for someone else? With great trepidation, and contrary to the advice he was given, he gave up his job at Pioneer Grain and accepted my offer that if he worked for me, I would give him the opportunity for partnership and shares in the company. I was fully aware that in order to grow the company sole ownership, I needed dependable people who had a vested interest in making it successful. My son, Darryl, was offered shares; George Wieler came on board because of the share offer; and Dale Heide, a young, aggressive and knowledgeable grain merchant from Saskatoon joined us under the same promise of partnership. We had an ambitious, resourceful team. All were customer service–oriented individuals. The business continued to grow exponentially, with a positive outlook for the future.

The best way to build a company is to surround yourself with people who have more to offer than you do—and who are smarter than you. And don't be afraid to relinquish some control. My philosophy of management has always been show me your competence and I will give you responsibility. Until that time, I will monitor your activities very closely—and yes, I have even been called a "micro manager."

By 2000, the company was well established, and we had almost reached the five-year mark that, statistically, was an indicator if a company would survive or fail. My banker was happy; the only loan I had outstanding was an operating loan, which increased dramatically, with no capital debt. All we needed to do was manage cash flow. To get to this point, my wife and I had given personal guarantees for $50,000 each. It was time to eliminate that and negotiate lower bank fees and interest rates. I started paying prime plus two points, but I continued to whittle away at those demands by always having another financial institution that was willing to take on our finances, even though in hindsight, changing financial institutions would have been a mistake. Eventually we had a flat fee account and a prime interest rate for our operating requirements. Our annual business had reached the $5-million mark, with more growth to come in the next five years.

In 2000, we were approached by United Grain Growers (UGG). Were we interested in purchasing the Mariapolis elevator just west of Highway 34, along the same Canadian National (CN) Railway line as Jordan? I was trying to make a case to CN that I could generate enough grain to maintain the short line. It was a much newer elevator and came with a manager who lived in the village. A problem arose with getting deliveries into and out of Mariapolis. Provincial road restrictions made truck hauling very limited, especially at a time when we were really counting on it. This issue would severely limit the future success of this facility and its contribution to Delmar's future.

One benefit that came out of purchasing the Mariapolis facility was learning from the elevator's exemplary modern design and replicating it in the Jordan facility. Mariapolis had an exposed elevation system on top of the roof, rather than internal confinement. In contrast, the Jordan facility was extremely difficult to keep clean as it was totally enclosed and had a high risk for fires and explosions. Sperling Welding got the job of doing a total makeover on the Jordan facility, ripping off the roof and the guts of the elevation system and replacing the former wooden legs and roof with steel. It resulted in a much-improved facility that was cleaner to operate and a leap into the modern era. This was a huge undertaking, and we spent close to three quarters of a million dollars on the old facility. Renovating the Jordan elevator in five years and paying for it with cash was pretty phenomenal. It proved to me that we were a company with a future.

Overhead at Delmar was very low, as was my personal salary, which left the money for bonuses to be distributed based on earnings. It's never a problem to pay out higher dividends if the money is there to do it. We began this company with few employees and a lot of hard work, then received and distributed the rewards from the profits to the shareholders and employees. We took our first annual trip as a company to Eagle Nest Resort (off Point du Bois) and included staff and management to review the year's past performance. We revisited that facility for fifteen years, with the exception of our tenth anniversary celebration, when we went to Vancouver Island for salmon fishing. It was not all grinding away at work; it came with fun, working together for a common cause.

* * *

One year previous, back in 1999, new life was breathed into the operation of the railway servicing our elevator when Southern Manitoba Railway bought the tracks from Morris going west past Mariapolis. This small-scale company was familiar, with a modest independent company like mine, which made our relationship flourish as we worked to achieve a common goal. I could never figure out why the Canadian government, responsible for railways across Canada, would ever entertain the idea of rail line abandonment, but a move in that direction was very much the norm. My concept was always why not create more flexibility by having CN and Canadian Pacific railways provide service on each other's lines, on a fee basis, using distance and payload as a guide? This way, if different destinations warranted the freight, they could compete with each other for fees or services. Less overhead, more dependability, more options. Instead, as short lines continue to be put up for sale, or simply abandoned, it creates additional stress on municipal and provincial road infrastructure, forcing even greater maintenance costs. I believe introducing these efficiencies would have been healthier for the grain companies and other shippers. The operation of the short line certainly started to improve my ability to compete in the rail destination markets.

The years 2000 to 2005 would see the biggest changes yet, preparing us for a future leap of faith. In 2001, we moved into a new office located in Winkler and bought the Somerset elevator from the newly formed Agricore group—the amalgamation of the pool and UGG, which changed some of the pool attitude and allowed me to negotiate a new terminal agreement if they sold me Somerset. That same year, we were contacted by another local pool board from Gladstone offering up that facility. I assumed it would be simple—I would offer them the same money I paid for Jordan—but it was not; however, that story is for another chapter. The years 2002 to 2003 became the story of a different venture, when Jordan Mills Inc. became a reality. Then along came 2004, with the riskiest decision in all of Delmar's history and likely its future: moving the La Rivière elevator intact to Somerset! In all of these cases, the opportunities simply came to our doorstep without us looking for them. I believe our customers saw us as a more viable opportunity to market grain than the establishment. If we ran into roadblocks, we either removed them or saw them coming and avoided them altogether. "Thinking outside the box" was what our team became known for, and we worked well together to accomplish the tasks.

Purchasing the Somerset facility went relatively smoothly. It was a newer facility on the former CN rail line, and owning it would boost our ability to help maintain the profitability of

A Booming Business

Southern Manitoba Railway. Now owning Jordan, Mariapolis and Somerset—that would surely be enough to provide the required volumes to keep the short line functional. The efforts were real and Southern Manitoba Railway was willing to help accomplish this, but bureaucracy was not on our side and certainly bigger established grain companies were not willing to offer support. Unfortunately, neither the federal government nor the provincial government were interested. The main rail industry fell under federal jurisdiction and the short lines fell under provincial jurisdiction, but neither had the vision to see what was happening to the industry.

During this era, the CWB started allocating cars on a tender basis, and the rail companies started offering incentives for twenty-five- and fifty-car unit trains. Our individual locations could not compete because we didn't have twenty-five or fifty car spots. Since the short line picked up the cars from CN at Morris, I assumed that if I could make a deal with the short line to accumulate and return a fifty-car unit from my three locations, I should be eligible for the incentive. The answer was a flat "No" from CN, and I was shocked at the reason why. It was not that we could not load the cars and return them to Morris in the required time; it was that the main rail lines were "forcing" larger facilities to accumulate a full fifty-car spot at one location. It would not be fair to them if they allowed me to load cars at multiple locations on a short line, regardless if the company was willing and we were able to deliver the cars to Morris as one unit. This made it clear that the "Big Boys" were not happy and wanted me out of their hair. Most locations being abandoned by the major companies were not made available to smaller upstarts but fell to the wrecking ball. It appeared the odds were stacked against us. As the CWB wanted to sell freight as a tender, I was basically pushed to tender. Because the bigger companies didn't participate, I got the tender every time. After a bit, I got wise to this. I quit discounting my bid and still received the cars I asked for. This move was short-lived though, and here the rest of the story takes a 180-degree turn into what ultimately made Delmar the success it became.

As this story unfolded, it became very clear that the norm would not be good enough to survive in this business; we had to be above the grade and have extraordinary ideas to be successful. I am so grateful for all the partners and staff, my banker and my accountant working together to make this happen.

EIGHTEEN:
The Deal Maker

For Delmar, 2001 was a tremendous year. We were in the middle of moving our office from the Jordan Corner to 915 Navigator Drive in Winkler. It started as a humble 1,000 square foot office, and it sure was cleaner than the office at Jordan. Making that move opened up a whole new dimension. So when I received a call from the Gladstone Pool Elevator Co-op board about their interest in selling their facility to Delmar, I was quite intrigued. My partner George Wieler and I discussed it; we were both attracted to the idea but didn't quite know how we would swing it. We offered them the same flat price of $150,000 I had paid for Jordan, plus I would give the members a two dollar per tonne premium for the crops they delivered. They turned me down and decided to go to tender. By that time, we were no longer invested, thinking we could not compete and feeling that our plate was pretty full. When we did not put in a tender as they expected, they called to ask if we were no longer interested. We were, but we had reservations. They wanted a full cash deal, no strings attached. George and I looked at the existing grain handling facilities in Manitoba and discovered that, other than a small facility at Holland owned by Patterson Grain, there was not another elevator still operating along Highway 34 from the U.S. border till Dauphin. So this location made sense. We decided, why not tender and lowball it? If we were to have it, well, we would. If not, well, that was fine too. We threw in a bid for $100,000 plus $1,000 for an empty lot adjacent to the elevator. I have no idea if we were the only bidder or if there were others, but we won the bid. The delays in the tender process meant that we could not have an August 1 possession. By the time the weigh-over was done, the elevator emptied and the keys handed to us, harvest was well underway.

I assumed the first year would be a bit slow. Since the members rejected my premium offer, I assumed they would also refuse to haul their grain to my elevator. My corporate year end was April 30, so this meant I would have less than nine months to see how this would work out in the current fiscal year. I had low expectations.

We hired the former Gladstone grain clerk and a manager from the pool at Killarney. It was a challenge, but they did a good job and fit in well with our other managers. We received some information from the pool's previous years and discovered that, in their best year, they handled 28,000 metric tonnes. This was a 6,000-tonne facility, the biggest we owned, and the rate of turns I was used to was at least seven per year. That meant it should handle approximately 42,000 tonnes per year. This would definitely be a future target. As it turned out, we handled 40,000 tonnes by April 30. When the dust settled, we had more than enough profit to pay for that entire investment in nine months! This gave us a huge boost in confidence to open up to other opportunities. We certainly would see more of them in the very near future.

* * *

In the spring of 2002, I had a visit from a friend of mine, Clarence Liescheid, who was interested in establishing a soybean crushing facility at Jordan Corner. We did the feasibility study, and it showed the market was available; at the time just over 10,000 acres of soybeans were grown in Manitoba. I did not want to put Delmar Commodities at risk, so I offered to partner but also seek other investors. Again, I went back into our established relationships and livestock growers to see if we could pull this off. This would be millions of dollars in investments that needed to be spread out. We had a number of information meetings. Some investors were not interested, but we had enough people with confidence to put together around $1.5 million in cash for shares with a guaranteed ten percent return. That seemed pretty aggressive; however, we were confident. Since I believed in local business support, we decided to finance the $500,000 balance from the local credit union. The projections were good and the capital in cash certainly more than adequate, so that's where I borrowed the money. Delmar would purchase the beans and sell the meal; Jordan Mills Inc. would receive the crush margins. It seemed like it was the answer. Delmar already had the sales team and storage facilities, so it was easy to divide the load.

This was where things got interesting. Manitoba Highways demanded we move the driveway leading to the mill away from the Junction of Highway 3 and Highway 23 because of concern that there were too many traffic accidents on that corner. That meant I would be buying a separate parcel of land north of the Junction and placing the turnoff just on the other side of a bridge crossing a creek. I think that was where my disrespect for Manitoba Highways originated. There was no common sense in this requirement! Slowing traffic in front of a bridge, on a road with a 100 kilometres per hour speed limit was unsafe and unreasonable. After considerable argument and disagreeing with their proposal, we came up with another option: create a driveway on Highway 23 just to the west of the elevator, get a joint access agreement with Delmar to build a small road leading to both facilities and completely close the existing access to Highway 3. Finally, Manitoba Highways agreed; we got the subdivisions done and the construction process began.

The process of doing the subdivision was simple, but it seemed onerous to send in the government-requested fifteen copies of the same information to the Manitoba Government Planning and Highways Department. I sent in three copies, assuming they had a photo copier to distribute the rest. Well, that was a mistake; it simply meant the file was rejected until I sent in the required number of copies. Lesson number one in dealing with the government.

Building a soybean crushing facility was a huge undertaking. Celerity Builders would put up the steel structure, Border View Electric would install the electrical, and the required equipment was ordered. But the process did not go off without a hitch. The construction trailer was broken into twice and all the tools, stolen. The first time, thieves stole older tools; two weeks later the stolen tools had been replaced with brand-new tools when crooks broke in again and stole the second batch. Not to be deterred, we carried on to completion and eventually a grand opening was held. Jordan Mills Inc. was a new company, and business started off with a whimper as we struggled to remove the oil from the meal coming through the presses. It was a challenge to sell inconsistently processed material to the hog industry, as it created a product with too much energy left in the feed. However, the extruders were such that no chemical was being used to extract the oil. Because there was no waste and the mill was run by hydroelectric power, the environmental impact was basically zero. The environmental approval process was a challenge because the Department of Oceans and Fisheries couldn't believe we had no waste and no chemical use.

There was a learning curve as we tried to determine if it was different varieties of beans that changed the soymeal makeup or if it was our presses that didn't work. Overhead was huge, as hydro rates were charged based on a demand meter reading, which meant we were paying for far more than we actually used. Our property taxes seemed high and labour costs were too high for our volume of production. This was a major concern—something needed to be done.

The plant was designed to buy product from a maximum radius of 100 miles and all the product could be sold within 100 miles. However, when the quality of the product was inferior to other soymeal, we attempted to sell it into the cattle market. Clarence tried to develop that market in Alberta, but shipping freight was a huge disadvantage compared to shipping it up from soymeal plants in the Upper Midwest United States. It became obvious this venture would not survive in the current format, so we looked at doubling the capacity to spread out the fixed costs. We could add an additional line—the hydro bill stayed the same, taxes were unchanged and the building size was adequate. All we needed to do was add about $300,000 worth of equipment to give us double the output. I approached the credit union where I financed the business and was flatly refused, even though we had over 50 percent cash equity and shareholders that could pay it out if needed. It made no difference. I needed to bring financials that showed a profit.

I knew that, under the credit union scenario, the purchase of new equipment would never happen, so I called Fred, my Delmar banker, to ask for his advice. His answer was quick.

While still on the phone, he said, "Go, give them a cheque and pay them out. We'll work this out!"

"Really," I said, "don't you want me to come in to apply?"

"Nope. You have an operating line, and if you're short, I'll cover it for you."

Here I remembered what I had learned earlier from my dad's dealings: just because the banker says you can do it, it doesn't make it the right thing to do, as the banker only looks at a balance sheet and the profits and doesn't understand your business. On the other hand, if someone has figured out how it can work and it makes perfect sense, don't walk away. There are great ideas and great people to carry out the ideas. The responsibility of proving that lies with the investor, as I had confirmed over and over again.

With the equipment expansion done and functioning, we still needed to find a way to correct the inconsistent quality of the soymeal. The oil was worth much more than the meal, so it was a double whammy, selling the meal for less because of the high oil content and having less oil to sell at the higher prices. We did have a clear freight advantage from the U.S. supplier. The freight spread taking beans down and the freight costs bringing meal back up was approximately fifty dollars per tonne. If all we did was capitalize on that spread, we would be profitable. Eventually it was accomplished, but not before Clarence got itchy feet and was looking at another venture. A group of investors in Northwood, North Dakota, wanted to build a crushing plant there and had huge grants available from the local and national government. In contrast, other than a small feasibility study grant, the facility at Jordan Mills was built without a cent from any government organization, and I liked that.

Northwood wanted Jordan Mills to be a shareholder; however, we were barely getting into the black and I didn't want to participate. Besides, we would lose a good chunk of the freight spread. The decision came down to Clarence selling his shares from Jordan Mills to Delmar. He proceeded to build the plant at Northwood with his partners from the North Dakota area. This proved to be unwise, as within a few years of operation, that whole facility became insoluble and was shut down. Later it was revived under another group, but that didn't work either, so today it is dismantled and mothballed. Lesson learned. If a business plan can't make it without a subsidy, the chances are slim it will ever make it with subsidies.

While Jordan Mills had location going for it in spades, it still faced a number of challenges. One was the inconsistent quality of the product, which resulted in an inability to separate the oil from the meal to create the saleable product. Another was that Jordan Mills shareholders did not want to carry any marketing risk, and since they did not have a marketing manager, they trusted Delmar to deal fairly in establishing trade values. Since I was involved as a principle in both companies, it was important to me to ensure both companies were treated fairly rather than Delmar pocketing easy money. Transferring beans between different companies with different owners was difficult to manage because of time-sensitive fluctuations in the price of the trades. Delmar bought the beans and sold the soybean meal and oil, and Jordan Mills received the crush margins. It was difficult to establish the value of the crush margins because of time lags and major market fluctuations.

An offer to sell Jordan Mills Inc. shares to Delmar Commodities Ltd. was made to the rest of the Jordan Mills shareholders. The shareholders were treated fairly; all them made money and Delmar took over the entire operation. This now became a streamlined, well-oiled machine; we no longer needed to duplicate services or be concerned about market fluctuations between trades. It was no longer a conflict of interest if Delmar exported beans to the United States and to the crush plant. My ethical dilemma was solved.

NINETEEN:
The Risk Taker

Grain marketing on a larger scale proved to be quite a challenge. Being a risk taker had its benefits; however, sometimes the risks were extremely high and, in hindsight, may have been very foolish. My company was doing most of the business on back-to-back trades. Since volumes would be available at a certain time but the markets to sell might not be, I could no longer manage my business by buying a few loads of grain from one source, then turning around and selling it to another. This meant I needed to set up a "futures" account with a commodity broker. That was not new to me as I was very familiar with that system, but I had to transition into an environment of "paper trading" instead of simply buying and selling individual loads.

In the meantime, in 2002/03, there were huge fluctuations in foreign exchange. As the business grew, hedging my grain became much more difficult as I proceeded to forward contract oats for fall and sell them for fall delivery, thinking I had locked in some pretty decent margins. Well, the value of the Canadian dollar skyrocketed between spring and the October/November delivery time, erasing every cent of margins and handing me a significant loss to the tune of a few hundred grand! I learned a valuable lesson. Bringing Dale Heide onboard to look after the "hedging" part of the business proved to be a huge asset for the company. Again, there are smarter people that just understand those specifics better than I do.

***

Not to be defeated, I ventured into another huge project. We were still trying to shore up grain capacity along the CN short line, including Somerset, and generate more deliveries to keep it a viable track. I heard the pool elevator at La Rivière was up for sale, so I connected with them to buy it. They refused to sell it to me, informing me that Anderson Building Movers from the Portage area was interested in purchasing it. I contacted the movers and we reached a deal. I would simply buy it "delivered and set up" at Somerset. This was the beginning of an unforeseen challenge. If only I had done a proper reference check ...

Our first questionable encounter came as Anderson requested the security payment; he said he needed it to pay a deposit to Manitoba Hydro for necessary services during the move. I understood and advanced him the money. When the time came, just before the move, he came up with the same line that Hydro asked for a cheque from me. Well, I paid that as a further advance. The next issue that arose was the need to take out an insurance policy in case the elevator fell over during the move. I only discovered this roadblock after we had spent over $250,000 on the base and concrete work at Somerset in preparation for the elevator delivery. This was no easy task since the engineering had to be done to support the huge structure with a foundation. This included making a pit twenty-four feet deep to accommodate the "leg" or elevation equipment, as well as an unloading pit to hold the grain. No turning back at this point.

Since the mover could not get insurance coverage for the move, I tried to purchase it on my own. I would not technically be the owner of the facility until it was delivered, so the agency chose not to sell me insurance coverage. So there we were, totally exposed to a risky mover and vulnerable to poor financial management. Plus, no insurance. The pressure and anxiety got the best of me. The move that would take a few weeks turned into a month, and I needed to take my mind off the project. Since I was not involved in the move itself, I chose a temporary reprieve, flying to San Antonio with Eleanor to see our daughter Lyn and her family. It was a great getaway, but we knew in time we would come home to face the facts of whatever would happen. This trip was more to preserve and prepare my state of mind for anything that would be thrown at me; it was not about having a "great escape." While preparing to catch our return flight, reality hit home. I received a call from Minty's Moving (who were subcontracted to make the move a success), informing me they had reached the correction line north of La Rivière. If I would not pay them before they crossed the main steel power line, they would drop the elevator right in the middle of the road!

I arrived home the next day and met with Anderson to inform him of the request from Minty's Moving and to bring yet another cheque to cover Anderson Building Movers' responsibility. Not having any legal paperwork in hand, I simply made him sign the copy of the cheque made directly to Minty, verifying that this was actually a portion of the balance I owed Anderson. He signed it, and the elevator continued its journey north to Somerset. The huge power line was crossed with lines dropped to the ground from the adjacent poles, never cut; they simply drove over the lines.

The day the elevator arrived in Somerset was a huge deal. Schools were dismissed to watch what would be a historic once-in-a-lifetime event for these kids. It reminded me a bit of the story of Jesus making His last trip to Jerusalem riding on a donkey, with the crowds out waving palm branches to celebrate this huge event. Of course, the elevator move did not, in any way, reflect the meaning of that biblical event, but I could sense an atmosphere of awe and privilege on the part of spectators at this unrivalled parade moving through the main entrance to Somerset and going right past the school.

If moving the facility was an art, Anderson Building Movers supplied the brawn and Minty's Moving provided the technical expertise. Reshaping the roads to get around corners and transporting the gigantic conglomerate of buildings over 130 feet high upright and across bumpy tracks to get to the site was a challenge. Up and down the hills the elevator was constantly being monitored with plumb lines to determine the tilt. This meant adjusting levelers or even adding blocking to level the elevator and prevent it from toppling over. In the end, moving the facilities up the hill and getting the necessary footing required additional trucks and caterpillars to make the final push.

Final adjustments were interesting to watch. The elevator crossed the rail line at a 45-degree angle by supporting the tilt with planking to keep it level. Finally, the last corner was maneuvered and the facility was placed intact on the prepared concrete foundation. The risk of toppling over was gone, with no insurance to claim and no issues, at least none that were visible to the TV crews from the History Channel following every step along the way. Minty's Moving had given them a heads up, on condition that credit for the move be focused on them. I am grateful that they did. As I stated, Minty was the one with the mental acuity to make this happen, without which this may well have been a totally different story. The responsibility to assemble the driveway, reposition the final resting place of the elevator with all the parts lining up and attach the office was part of the agreement with Anderson for the cost of delivery. After waiting and prodding Anderson for a few months, I realized he wasn't going to make this happen and I had to hire a new contractor to finish the work. I did not pursue any legal action, as I knew there was no possibility of payment. I would simply move on, cover the extras and start using this wonderful facility.

During this time, the rumour mill was alive and well. Allegedly, one of Anderson's creditors was told that if I would pay my bill with Anderson, he would pay his creditor. I received a call from a concerned brother, asking if I had not paid Anderson. While this story had the capacity to severely damage the historical record I had established, the Somerset facility, with the most potential and flexibility, became the best we had. In the year to come, the move was aired on the History Channel as one of the World Mega Moves—from highlighting the London Airport Control Tower, moved with precision by robots, to the guts and mud move of our facility from La Rivière to Somerset. Eventually the rumours were also laid to rest.

Just as this awe-inspiring building was not dropped in the middle of the road, nor did it topple while crossing railroad tracks, these issues did not break me or my company. God continued to provide very generously, above what we expected or deserved. Daily I am grateful that I could draw on God's grace and endless provision while dealing with a very volatile situation. And I continue to learn and to give and accept forgiveness.

* * *

Elevators intact, staff in place to run the facilities, a great accounting system from Thede Ward to track the day-to-day activities including the financials, with CWB reconciliation similar to what ConAgra used for their company—I felt pretty good. We were ready to really bring Delmar Commodities Ltd. to another level, more accurately serving a larger number of customers. While the Canadian Wheat Board was still in operation, issues with the CWB were getting extremely frustrating for the free marketing ConAgra to be around, at least that's how it seemed to me. ConAgra gave up the wait in 2005, when they decided to sell off the four country facilities they owned to J.R. Richardson and Sons. It meant the head office in Winnipeg would adjust to being a marketing arm for CWB grain, which was a bit of a joke in my view. Why would the likes of the CWB, claiming to be such an essential component of a sole marketing desk for farmers, even need the likes of ConAgra or the Cargills of the world? So, as it turned out, we really didn't have that much to do with them other than engaging the services of William Van Osch to assist us in doing our monthly financial statements and CWB reconciliation reports. That connection would lead us to another very interesting opportunity.

As ConAgra wound down, it seemed William would be the "last man standing" in Canada to turn the lights out when the office later closed the doors. He was left reconciling the CWB country inventory balance including any other cleanup—like office furniture. Our earlier connection prompted William to approach us and ask whether we were interested in assuming the ConAgra liabilities with the CWB. There were literally thousands of tonnes of CWB feed wheat, including malt and feed barley liabilities. This happens when a company has shipped grain out as their own inventory due to quality issues or if a company has shipped one grade of grain, but it is downgraded at the destination because it doesn't meet the standard at which it was shipped. In some cases, the grain simply had to be disposed of with the hope of replacing it later. That was the way the system worked, but what was purchased on the board's account had to be delivered to their account. In my case, as I am sure it was with everyone who was an agent of the CWB, they would pay me for the inventory I bought on their account and pay me storage until the grain was shipped. It was a sweet deal because, if I was running short on operating line to finance my non-board activities, I would switch to push for CWB deliveries and collect their storage fees. Once we officially took over the CWB liabilities, the storage money would immediately flow to Delmar. I often said we were collecting "air miles" on this grain, because we didn't actually have it all in inventory, but this set the stage for the opportunity to make good money on the positions we inherited from ConAgra. The new space at Somerset became an instant storage paycheque every month. What happened over the next while would reinforce the move we made and produce some tremendous upcoming opportunities.

La Rivière elevator ready to move to Somerset on TV's "The World Mega Moves"

A Scrappy Little Nobody

La Rivière elevator on the road, up the hills and around the corners over hydro lines to Somerset

TWENTY:
The Movers and Shakers

Media coverage of moving the elevator hit international levels, business was booming and new opportunities kept surfacing. The impact that taking on ConAgra's CWB liabilities had on Delmar's success in business over the next few years would surprise us.

Canada was a quality supplier of wheat and malt barley, and the Canadian Grain Commission (CGC) was in place to ensure that standards on Canadian exports were met. Domestic brewers were assured of quality. International markets were taught how to use our wheat and could likewise depend on the value when it was delivered. The CGC ensured that grain company liabilities to farmers were "somewhat guaranteed"; therefore, the grain industry needed to be licensed and bonded. The bond was generally secured by a letter of credit from the bank that was financing the company being protected. As a smaller company, it was extremely difficult for Delmar to acquire a bond big enough to satisfy all outstanding cheques at every month end. Many times, we exceeded our limit, especially once farmers started to ask for "deferred" cheques as they dealt with excess income for one year and needed that income in the following year. Technically, the cheques could be outstanding for half a year; however, the CGC guaranteed them for a maximum of just three months. I doubt if many producers really understood the risk they took. The important thing was to deal with reliable companies that were trustworthy. That is what our goal and objective was: not to be the biggest or the most popular but to be a company that was dependable and trustworthy. The cost of getting the line of credit was becoming too high and the limits it placed on our borrowing capacity to finance the grain, too harsh. We finally found an insurance company that the CGC would accept, and we no longer needed a letter of credit. That was a game changer. Even though we still needed to do the monthly reporting, our premiums were simply adjusted with plenty of fluidity to meet our needs, expanding our ability to grow and meet the legal obligations to the CGC.

This move allowed us to prepare for some tremendous opportunities waiting at our doorstep. Since we absorbed the ConAgra CWB liabilities, we were required to buy wheat from the farmers and ship it to the CWB account. We were already involved in trade with flour millers in the United States and were shipping wheat there, fully aware of the opportunities to fetch more money for these markets. Some of them preferred truck deliveries, which fit into our company objectives for service. The railways were getting more and more difficult to deal with.

It was fall, and the initial payment for wheat was around five dollars per bushel. However, the milling market in the United States was trading for twenty-two to twenty-three dollars per bushel. The U.S. Marshall Wheat variety was much higher yielding than our Canadian Red Spring varieties, so farmers were switching to growing Marshall Wheat even though it was considered a Canadian feed wheat. So here is where I saw an opportunity: buy the Marshall feed wheat on the non-board side and fill my obligations to cover my short position with the CWB; then buy it back from the board as feed wheat, get a permit from them and ship it to my U.S. flour mills, which had no issue with using Marshall Wheat, as that was the most common variety they used. We covered more than enough for my CWB liabilities, and we had enough non-board wheat to add some surplus to the board. We now actually owned more wheat than we owed them.

As we kept shipping literally hundreds of truckloads south, the margins were big and we had already been paid storage for more than a year. For Delmar, it became the highlight financially. From the farmers' perspective, they saw we could offer them an opportunity and reward them accordingly. This continued long enough for the non-board market to reflect that we paid a producer in Western Manitoba twenty-one dollars per bushel for his Marshall Wheat, picked up on his farm, at a time when he would have had to sell this perfectly good milling wheat to the board as feed—or into the hog and poultry feed market for less than half that money.

* * *

I also had barley liabilities to the CWB from the ConAgra deal, which took a bit longer to resolve. I really didn't care that it took another year; after all, the CWB was paying storage revenue. Since the malt barley market was much more active in Alberta and they were having a bumper crop, I resolved my problem by transferring my liabilities to Providence Grain Solutions. This became the reverse of the ConAgra deal, where Providence Grain was "long" to the CWB.

The term "long" may be a bit of odd to the average reader, so here's an explanation. Whenever a company bought a tonne of grain on behalf of the CWB, the company owed the CWB that tonne of grain including the grade—they were never in a positive or negative position. When a grain company couldn't meet those obligations, it became a liability that they paid for or someone could choose to accept the liability from the grain company, replace it with grain they bought as non-board grain and ship it to them. In my case, I chose to accept the barley liabilities from ConAgra, but I struggled to find the correct quality of barley to ship. One day, I got a call from Milt Miller, a friend who used to work with me at Cargill in Elm Creek and who had started Providence Grain Solutions in Alberta. He asked me if I would be willing to make a deal and transfer my liabilities to him. Milt was also an agent of the CWB; he bought non-board barley that met the malt standards and then shipped it to Vancouver on the CWB account. This meant he needed CWB liabilities to cover his non-board purchases—he needed to be in an opposite situation than I was. You could say he was "long" or had shipped too much non-board to the CWB. Well, I approached the CWB, explained I was struggling to find the right quality of barley and applied to transfer the liabilities I took from ConAgra to Providence Grain. Both Milt and I ended up happy. As it turned out, I ensured myself a good margin and received storage revenue for a few years, plus I eliminated shipping costs all the way to Vancouver!

There are several reasons why I think that story belongs in this book. I never believed the CWB was that smart, and I never believed they really were there to give farmers the best opportunities. Instead, the CWB became a bureaucracy simply concerned about the status quo. I have never understood how farmers believed they were getting the best options when, many times, I was able to get more or different opportunities not ever pursued by the board. Yes, I figured out how the CWB operated and where the blind spots were that they never tracked down. I recall making inventory adjustments with the board to match market grade spreads that suited my situation and having the capability to adjust them back on another year end to facilitate market changes. My company was very "small peanuts" compared to other companies that had the same opportunities.

The driving factor for the CWB existence was to equal the playing field for every producer in Western Canada, but this eliminated the ability to sniff out regional market opportunities. Perhaps there was no motivation, not even a vision to do that; they had a guaranteed source of grain, and it didn't matter if they screwed up because the gains and losses were all hidden in their so-called "pool" account. Delmar was not a big company relative to the other grain giants—or perhaps I could refer to them as "elephants." CWB was the biggest of them and not easily moved. Thinking of my company being referred to as a little "mouse" and easily trampled, I took up the challenge to simply be that mouse. By the time they figured out what I was up to, I was doing something completely different. I prefer to call that flexibility.

* * *

It was 2006, and Delmar was celebrating ten years of a very demanding but successful business. We now employed over twenty individuals whose families depended on their paycheques. It was a huge responsibility from my perspective. We had won awards from *Manitoba Business Magazine* (including recognition for Jordan Mills) as the fastest growing company. I recall us standing next to Jennifer Jones, a young lawyer and world-famous curler representing a well-established legal firm that was also a contender for this award. We beat them out and won top honours! We had amalgamated Jordan Mills and Delmar to become a company to be reckoned with, a business with over $30 million per year in sales.

A Scrappy Little Nobody

* * *

I made another promise to my wife. I would take the year off to contemplate what the next steps would be, but again, I had no idea how that would turn out. The partner group was eager to take on more responsibility, which would free me up.

In January 2006, I took the opportunity to travel to India with Children's Camps International to experience and support the children's camping ministry. Those two weeks helped me understand the culture of India and the challenges facing that camping organization. I was introduced to some unfamiliar foods and so employed an approach that involved taking along a few boxes of cheese crackers in case I went hungry. I consumed them all!

After two weeks, I came home for a week, as my daughter was expecting a child, but by February 2, I was back on a plane to India—this time with the Gideons International organization and no new baby yet. While in the Toronto airport, I got the call: I had a new grandson! The excitement and joy of seeing and meeting him would be delayed until my return in another two weeks.

My experience in India for a full month was life changing, not only by being exposed to another culture but also in seeing the miracles of God in this vibrantly alive and diverse country. I realized He is not limited to working only in the Western world or any particular hemisphere.

To add further excitement to our lives, Eleanor and I decided we would join Back to the Bible (at that time under the direction of Woodrow Kroll) to experience the State of Israel from a biblical perspective. This was a challenge as Eleanor was at risk of a lupus flare-up when exposed to sunshine, and we certainly would need to limit the amount of walking she did. We put out a prayer request to our local church, family and friends and left for Israel the middle of March. It was a phenomenal experience. After that trip, reading the Bible became so alive and more enlightening, having discovered and actually stood on the ground where Jesus may have walked.

We had an awesome two weeks in Israel and added a Mediterranean cruise to wrap it up, with a stop at Ephesus in Turkey, the Island of Patmos and, of course, Athens, Greece.

* * *

How can you come home to normal after several months of "amazing" and realize that it's only April? What would the rest of the year look like?

Delmar Commodities was doing well and the team was gelling according to plan. I was busy that summer attending different functions, mowing my grass, mowing my grass and mowing my grass. Yes, boredom was setting in! It was an election year for Winkler City Council and I had been saying, "No," to running for council and for mayor—numerous times—until the middle of August when I remembered the motto: "Go where you think there is a need and where people are asking you to consider that need."

Following discussions with Eleanor, my family and my business partners, where I asked them what they thought, I was convinced I should give the mayoral race a shot. After all, it was in Winkler that Dr. Cornelius Wiebe had given me a chance at life; what would be wrong with running for mayor in Winkler? I was asked, "What do you know about running a city? You have not even been a councillor and they have an eight-million-dollar budget. You need to run for councillor first, then perhaps mayor." Well, if you have read my story to this point, you will know that I prefer to lead; I feel that is where my gifts lie. I checked out the process with Vince

Anderson, chief administrative officer of the city, and he gave me the paperwork to get signatures.

A number of wise people told me you have to go to the "Who's Who" in Winkler to get signatures. Again, I was just learning the ropes, but I thought it was more important to connect with the people I would be serving than to gain prominence. I left city hall and began walking down Main Street to collect thirty signatures, planning to end up at the Delmar office to finish up, as I had earlier told my son, Darryl, that I wanted him to sign the nomination papers. By the time I got partway down Main Street, I had more than enough signatures; I had to turn the page over to have my son and some staff sign the papers before bringing them back to city hall. And so, a three-way race for the mayor's seat began. One contender was a former councillor; the other, a former economic development officer; and me ... risk taker, deal maker, mover and shaker.

I could not substantiate any issues the previous council had, but that really didn't matter to me. I was simply giving people the choice of who they wanted to lead the city. I was my own financier, promotional department and advertising agent! I actually put up my own signs. I didn't want to obligate anyone to vote for me because they owed me something or to owe anyone anything and have them expect favours from me.

The draw was made for placement on the ballot and I was in the middle. I decided to take that ballot as the format for my advertising campaign, fading the other two names and bolding my name in the middle with a one-liner: "The Clear Choice." This became the buzz word, and when election day rolled around, I made only two promises: I would ensure Bethel Heritage Park became a reality on the former Bethel Hospital site, and when Frank Reimer asked what I would do for him, I said jokingly but with some determination, I would work toward getting rid of his old, rat-infested elevator in the middle of town. We laughed about it because he knew that was a problem.

Voting was to take place in the elementary school gym. The day of the election, I was informed I could be present in the lobby to say hi to the voters and thank them for coming to vote. After watching people speak to both of my opponents, I called my wife, telling her, "I don't think this will work. I won't become mayor." When the polls closed, I attended the count as a candidate, and after watching the count for about twenty minutes, seeing my vote pile accumulating rapidly, I called Eleanor again to inform her I likely would become mayor! People supported my nomination beyond what I could ever have hoped for. I received 67 percent of the votes, with the other two candidates receiving 33 percent together. I had no agenda, just a willingness to serve, which I had demonstrated to the people as Chamber of Commerce president and by serving five years as Harvest Festival director. I actually cared for this city and had invested significant time to improve the quality of life in Winkler, with no personal agenda.

TWENTY-ONE:
In the Mayor's Chair

The election results were a bit overwhelming. I never thought a win would be possible, but now came the next chapter of what I was going to do. My Delmar office remained in place; however, I became less and less involved in the daily operations. My banking systems were changed in order for me to see my bank accounts online at the office—and as they say, you never really make money until it's recorded in your bank account. So, the transition was relatively easy. I was just going to have an additional office to go to.

My first day in the mayor's chair was somewhat frantic, as I don't think anyone had expected me to win the election. The office space was in a bit of turmoil—actually I would be sitting in the back of a storage room while renovations were being done. Eventually a new office emerged, complete with a small table and chairs, where I met with visitors. Since I loved sales and marketing, I felt it was important to understand the needs in the community and the functionality of the City of Winkler operations. I was the ex-officio of every committee, and in order to learn the system, I attended every committee meeting, making the job much more time consuming than simply being a "public figure" for the city. I learned so much and actually felt like I could have input all around. I know for some it may have been too much, but I was determined not to be sideswiped and highjacked by committees. We would get together for discussion and find solutions together. I was not afraid to share ideas that I thought were important. So, you can say I jumped in with both feet and made the mayor's chair a higher priority than running Delmar.

My first conflict arose with the operations of the Harvest Festival. Technically, it fell under the umbrella of the Business Improvement Area (BIA) board and the Winkler and District Chamber of Commerce, but there were some issues that city council needed to address. Old Time Value Days, once run as a downtown business promotion, had changed with the establishment of the Harvest Festival and the addition of the Southland Mall in 1985. I felt this needed to be a City of Winkler celebration event. I didn't think the Chamber of Commerce needed to put all their efforts into running a city celebration at the expense of neglecting the businesses they were supposed to support. After all, the Chamber was a business-run organization designed to support and assist the business community. My idea was that the city's role was to create an environment where businesses flourish, and the Chamber's role was to help them ensure they were successful.

The other issue needing to be addressed was efficiency and duplication. As it stood, the BIA received the business tax portion and simply handed that money to the Chamber to run the festival. Why would the City of Winkler collect business taxes for the BIA simply to have them write one big cheque to the Harvest Festival and that was about the only reason that group existed? Why not have the Harvest Festival expenses paid directly by the city instead of going through two other organizations?

Plans were made to have the Harvest Festival function as an organization reporting to the City of Winkler. That idea went over like a lead balloon. Some individuals who were leading it thought they would have a standoff and threatened to resign. Well, I had experienced this move before. If there had been a legitimate reason to change our plans, we may have considered it, but threats without a solution just didn't work for me. So we called their bluff. Not to make this a vendetta, we added more volunteers who were willing to work as a community and open to a new way of doing things. To be a follower, I need not be in the mayor's chair. I assumed people wanted a visionary and I was about to deliver. To answer a question that was posed to me........"What did someone with business experience have to offer to the city?"—I believe the lessons learned on my own dime would prove to be very valuable to bring to the city council table.

The next big challenge right out of the gate was fulfilling my promise to deliver a park at the former Bethel Hospital site, now owned by the city. There was already a monument there, a "postage stamp cairn" placed in the southeast corner to commemorate, as part of local history, the early Jewish settlers' impact on the retail component of Winkler. The city "committees" had previously decided that the rest of this property would become the location for a much-needed new fire hall as well as a police station, also much needed. However, there was simply no other place in the entire city as well suited to a park as this location. My argument was, we have a city with no downtown destination point and no park between Mountain and Pembina all the way from 15th Street to Highway 32. The city was more than a conglomerate of public facilities; it needed an outdoor place for people to relax that could become a place of meeting. Their next idea was that it should actually become a housing project, generating money from the builder, whoever that might be. Again, that simply did not fly.

One day, my city manager at the time, the chief administrative officer, called a council meeting to make a final decision regarding the former Bethel Hospital property. I was not aware of his intentions, but the fact that he was under pressure by other staff to secure this property once and for all did not sit well with me. I had no other site, but I had not exhausted all options and did not realize the urgency. In any case, we were at the meeting when the proposal came forward. I was not familiar with the procedure, but I thought, at the very least, as the mayor, I would be informed what the meeting was for before I got there. When he told Council we would have the final vote, I got up and said that there would be no vote that day. I wanted two weeks to study the options further.

Meanwhile, the Horticultural Society and the Heritage Society were both pushing for a park, and they knew I was also promoting it. I pondered the options. Essentially, I had a bare cupboard because any suggestion I made was dismissed. I sat in my office trying to figure this out when a phone call came from David Hamm, pastor of the Cornerstone Church. Their congregation had bought the former Rhinelander Church building on Pembina Avenue (a location that was basically one block closer to Highway 32 and across the road from the property in question). The Cornerstone Church was offering to do a swap with the old fire hall building on 4th Street. They would remove the building, leaving bare land, and we would offer them the old fire hall, a lot for parking (shared with the credit union) plus a $200,000 cheque.

What a relief when Bill Zacharias, the city engineer, informed me that the lot was exactly the size needed for the newly proposed fire hall building! Council agreed, the deal was made and both parties were happy. Looking back today, I am still amazed at how this transaction was completed within the two weeks I requested, that council agreed to proceed and that the fire chief was happy as well! It is gratifying when things come together. The final result has served to put Winkler more prominently on the map—an attractive city venue with fire protection available on a much larger scale. This opened the door to a great service partnership with the RM of Stanley, including a formal fire protection agreement we still appreciate.

The Bethel Heritage Park Building committee began in earnest to secure designs for the work and content of the park. In time, construction began. Such a work of dedication, supported by a public fundraiser that raised over $1.5 million in less than eight months, made this project so very successful. Community businesses as well as individuals were firmly behind this project.

We did have one local adversary who continued to call and send emails saying that our project, with a Bethesda Fountain and angels as well as a brick wall with scripture dedicated to conscientious objectors, was in violation of his human rights in this city. In his mind, this matter needed to be addressed and the items he objected to, removed. I was very gentle; however, I made it clear that this was truly a heritage project and, whether he liked it or not, this was a part of our history. (Besides, there is a Bethesda Fountain at Central Park in the centre of New York City. The two are an exact replica of each other, only the Winkler one is much nicer with the marble!) This response did not suffice, and he proceeded to file a formal statement of claim against the City of Winkler, the Horticultural Society and the Heritage Society. This was serious stuff. What now? I had a friend, Art Stacey, working as a lawyer for Thompson Dorfman Sweatman in Winnipeg, who I got to know while working toward establishing a business in Winkler. I had a conversation with him, and he informed me that he would be very willing to take on this case to represent the City of Winkler. I sent all my documented conversations with the concerned individual

In the Mayor's Chair

to the lawyer. With that information, the City of Winkler and the co-accused were exonerated, and the case was dismissed.

But the chapter on the promised park was not yet complete; there would be more! We had built the fire hall at another location, and now we needed to get ready to build a new police station. The previous council had taken the much-needed step to establish a war veterans cenotaph behind city hall. It was great, but it almost seemed hidden, as if we were not quite comfortable with it. As the park was being developed, I had a conversation with Harvey, a businessman friend of mine, about the possibility of moving this cenotaph to the new park next to Main Street. He thought that, from a visibility perspective, that would be awesome, but to have it in the new park would be "unbelievable." He proceeded to follow protocol and made an application to the provincial veterans' organization to move the cenotaph. They turned it down—no real reason, but they did not approve.

Not taking "No" for an answer, Harvey suggested we could appeal this decision to the national veterans in Ottawa. Again, we received a negative response. However, this time I wanted an explanation as to why. It turned out it wasn't only the Mennonite conscientious objectors who had issue with the veterans; the veterans had an equal hang up about being in the same park as the conscientious objectors! This led to conversations between the veterans and Harvey and me as I explained to them the makeup of the Bethel Heritage Park. Dialogue ensued about how this community had struggled for years with war veterans, including church discipline for those members that went to war. By now, the circumstances had changed, and as a community we wanted to heal the rift. I explained to them that if they looked at the park design, they would see that veterans would be given prominence on Main Street. Bethesda Fountain, a biblical reference to a "healing fountain," would stand between war veterans and conscientious objectors, representing the healing taking place over the past sixty years. Was it not time to put that painful part of history behind us?

The answer we got back was "Yes, go ahead and move the cenotaph!" We followed through with all the protocols and made it happen.

* * *

This was all first-term stuff, not the normal way to start a mayoral term, but it did work. If I had not become personally involved in these situations, I doubt that I would have been motivated to carry on. But I saw the results, I knew what it took to get it done, and yes, there was that element of feeling satisfied. I had done a good job!

Frank Reimer's elevator, as promised, was a first-term demolition. But what became interesting as it was being dismantled, similar to all the other old elevators, was that this elevator didn't fall down as planned. Due to some spoiled grain hanging up in one of the overhead bins, the centre of gravity was not correctly calculated, and it smashed right over the railroad tracks (with residents watching), almost hitting the fence on the north side lining their condo complex! And as expected, literally dozens of rats scurried for shelter before being hunted down.

TWENTY-TWO:
The Office of Choice

Holding down the fort in the mayor's chair did not prevent Delmar from continuing to expand, even though sometimes it may have seemed that we would be severely hindered from growing. In 2007, a year after being elected mayor, Southern Manitoba Railway pulled up stakes (literally) and abandoned the only rail line that served Jordan, the new Somerset facilities. I had sold the Mariapolis facility to Canada Malt in a continued effort to shore up the traffic on that line. It seemed all that work and benefit would be lost due to this decision to abandon.

It became obvious that there was only one solution: we had to transport all this grain to the end user and big terminal destinations by truck. Trucking it was, and as we continued to pursue every avenue to put this plan into action, it turned out to be the best year Delmar ever had in its history. Overall, rail movement became burdensome. We shipped out of Gladstone because it was still serviced by CN; it was also a convenient way for other grain companies to access a quick source of grain when their railcars arrived and they needed grain fast to fill them. Otherwise, our efforts to build up the truck service business were successful, and it literally exploded! I have learned that as one door closes another one opens.

Cash flow requirements had accelerated, including my operating line at the bank. I was still being served by the same RBC bank and manager (Fred Stock), but now the pressure was on to take out a capital loan to finance my assets rather than using only my operating line—because their "ratios" didn't work out. I didn't know that much about ratios, but I did know we had a sufficient operating line and the company continued to show healthy profits, so why would I need a separate loan for my assets? Finally, I succumbed to their wishes and took out a loan, not a mortgage, because I refused to add legal and mortgage costs to my expenses. I guess that was my compromise. However, in the fall, as farmers were deferring their cheques into the new year, I literally had millions in cash sitting in my chequing account. I looked on my screen and noticed I was paying interest on my capital loan but getting nothing from the balance in my chequing account. As Fred got his next month-end report from the bank, he called in a panic.

"Martin, what did you do?"

Obviously, my ratios didn't measure up to their expectations! It was such a nice feeling when I clicked a mouse on the screen and saw my asset loan paid in full, with cash in the bank! I had that feeling of freedom, similar to what I felt when paying off my house mortgage fifteen years earlier. I believe this was a sign that my tolerance for taking chances was starting to fade and perhaps I should reduce my risks.

With the grain business fully in high gear, we began looking for other opportunities to build the business; at the same time, we had other companies starting to sniff around for what it would take to buy us out.

By 2009/10, it became obvious to me that I might be interested in exiting the business. At the same time, we had grown this company to an annual sales volume of over $50 million. It had become a bit of an attraction to potential buyers. I had some U.S. interest in trying to purchase the entire company, to the point where we had reached a tentative agreement with a significant deposit, subject to "due diligence." We started the process in October 2008. It dragged out till the end of December and extended multiple times, till the close of our corporate year, April 30. Well, that time passed as we waited for our official financial results from the accountant, plus their review. Again, the date was extended, this time to the end of June.

My family had holiday plans for July, and I wanted this wrapped up before we left, so I simply informed them I wanted the closing date to remain June 30, 2008. Our agreement stated that if they backed out, I kept the deposit; however, if I backed out, I would return their deposit, plus all my costs to get to this point would be mine. In my opinion, the company had plenty of time to close the deal and I had been very patient. This notice, however, spooked them, and they informed my lawyer that they were backing out of the deal because I was too pushy! That was not how I saw it. Since I did not back out, I kept the deposit according to the agreement. Being an American company, the buyers thought that we Canadians didn't quite measure up and they demanded I send their deposit back. I learned an important lesson that day: make sure your ducks are in a row and you have a solid legally binding agreement in place. That action authorized us to keep the deposit; in fact, I paid most of the deposit money out to my accountants and lawyers who helped get us to this point. Without the ability to understand the Canadian system or appreciate the values of Delmar Commodities, I don't believe the company that had hoped to purchase Delmar would have survived financially in Canada. It could have been another Southern Manitoba Railway–type of abandonment and disassembling of structures.

A Scrappy Little Nobody

Delmar was not done; business continued to grow as we extended our search to get into the soybean seed business. That would fit well into our overall market plan to provide a quality seed to supplement the soybean crushing business. In the meantime, I had a visit from a group of local business partners that operated Keystone Grain in Winkler. These guys were very familiar with our business and thought it would fit well with what they were doing at Keystone. They were in the mood to sell off Keystone and they already had a buyer, so our negotiations began in earnest. But this time, I had no intention of putting my partners through agony again, so I informed the potential buyer that I would sell exactly 50 percent of Delmar and would not expose my partners to losing control of the company we had built up. The deal was made. I sold six percent of my shares to my kids and to another great employee, Mark Jorgensen, who was in charge of product sales for the crushing plant. I had promised him an opportunity to buy shares, and as I was going to step aside, this seemed to be the time. Annual sales at this point reached over $65 million, and we employed twenty-eight people. Selling the business would prepare me to commit and give full-time attention to the mayor's chair. Both my own and my wife's shares would be sold.

Now the family members still involved at Delmar were my daughter Rhonda, who was a silent shareholder (though her husband worked there), and my son, Darryl, who began this journey with me. The rewards at this point, compared to the expectations of the original failed attempt at selling the company, proved to be beyond my wildest dreams. We began this company in 1995 and to reach this point of success by 2011 was unheard of; I continue to thank God for the opportunities to work with great partners who have been largely responsible for the growth of this company. I could never have accomplished this on my own. Without them, I would have continued to be that "Rinke-dink" in the grain business.

* * *

The business skills I learned continued to be an asset as I served in the mayor's chair, and they allowed me to help other small local businesses start up and grow their company. These skills also made it possible for me to set up Eleanor and myself financially so we could build a new home with all the frills we wanted, incorporating "the cottage we never wanted" into the design and size of our beautiful new house. This would be our "forever" home. But, as we would discover only three years later, our forever home would be very temporary for Eleanor.

Having more time meant I could get involved as a central district representative serving the larger region on the board of the Association of Manitoba Municipalities (AMM), a municipal lobby group that focuses on representing all Manitoba municipalities (including the cities) to the Manitoba government. The experience was awesome. However, I quickly learned that I didn't like "lobbying," as I had very little patience for political games, and that's what I saw. It did seem that there was an avenue for some AMM board members (especially the executive group) to have the ear of Manitoba cabinet ministers, which resulted in funding for projects in their respective communities. I am not convinced it reached down to the rest of us, so the posturing got a bit tiring. I realized I was not cut out to stroke a politician's ego. I guess that did cause some stress and may have resulted in some disagreements. My common-sense approach to finding solutions was difficult to promote in those circles.

I did get some appointments on committees where I served, including the Manitoba Justice Advisory Council. I served five years on that board and gave a lot of suggestions, but I really don't think we achieved a single thing! The other group I served with was the Manitoba Accessibility Council, and there, we got involved in making recommendations that resulted in a document for legislation to follow. My role on that committee was to bring common sense, practical solutions that could be implemented rather than watching legislation coming out of it, with little in the way of realistic, affordable solutions. I was pleased that, by the time I left that group, significant progress had been made for reasonable accessibility regulations.

The experience itself served us well, but it seemed futile when it came to the establishment of "police boards" that no one wanted and municipal amalgamation being shoved down municipalities' throats without consultation. In addition, I observed that some municipalities struggled a lot with internal bickering and shady procedures that we, as the AMM, should address. But I was informed that was not our mandate. I wondered, "Why not?" These issues had resulted in municipal disarray, and temporary managers had to come in, time and time again, to sort things out at great expense to the taxpayer. I could not solve that, no matter how hard I tried. I could not solve the issue of the abandonment of chemical use to control weeds in towns, due to legislative changes and many other issues. The extra costs to municipalities that tried using alternative chemicals was more than triple the cost of using federally approved products. What I did accomplish, and why I hold my head up high, is that I brought issues to the table regarding my struggles with speed zone management by municipalities and the fact that bus line routes were enshrined in the Motor Transport Board, regardless if those routes were no longer being serviced. In response, the government in power actually dismantled those two boards, and the ability to determine speed zones in communities was returned to the municipalities.

TWENTY-THREE:
The Best-laid Plans

Four terms in the mayor's office: in 2006, my bid was contested; in 2010, I was acclaimed; in 2014, I had one opponent, Wolfgang Schaefer; and in 2018, I was again acclaimed as mayor.

The year 2014 saw excitement kindled in the community by the growth boom in Winkler. Businesses were expanding and new developers were building multifamily units. At the Senior Centre, discussions were ongoing. This centre owned the property where the Buhler Active Living Centre was to be built. The seniors were concerned was about giving up their space as well as their main source of income coming from these rentals. (The candidate running against me was one of their regular renters, so that made it even tougher.) Their main user paid them a thirty-dollar rent, which obviously wouldn't pay the bills in the new building. So, our offer was to buy their property at appraised value, then develop a seniors' centre inside the Buhler Active Living Centre. Hearing all the stories of what could go wrong, there was a growing discontent among the seniors. In their minds, we were taking away their property, even though they were getting full market value.

In another area of the city, at the corner of Highway 14 and Roblin Boulevard, a new developer was planning a major multi-storey, multi-unit development, located between the highway and an existing higher-end development. They thought we were bringing "sub-level" housing into an upscale neighbourhood. The seniors and property owners in that area were against me, regardless of our promises of a great development coming. Most complaints were about property values deteriorating, too much traffic, and that attracting residents and commercial property in that corner was not right. I began to feel a bit nervous; I had not been in that situation before, and it felt like I had lost all my friends.

* * *

In the summer, Eleanor's health took a turn for the worse. She had struggled with lupus for twenty-seven years and, as a result of immune deficiency, had suffered with shingles on two occasions in her life. The first major episode was in August 1997 (the exact time of Princess Diana's fatal car crash). I knew what that was like for her; the second time would turn out to be much worse. In August 2014, after receiving a shingles vaccine, she contracted another bout. After numerous doctor visits, with no relief or solutions, I took her to emergency at Boundary Trails Hospital; this time it was Dr. Hennie Basson on duty. He saw the severity of the shingles, coupled with the fact that she had lupus, and decided that she needed to be admitted. It was so good to have someone care enough to try to help. I thought it would be a short-term stay of a week or two. It turned out to be the last time she ever left our home. It was devastating to watch. Knowing there was a very distinct possibility I would face this mayoral term alone, I had a difficult decision ahead of me: should I run for another term or just hang it up?

The Best-laid Plans

Eleanor and I discussed at length how this might work. Then she looked up and said, "Martin, you have to carry on and win this election. The city needs you." Her confirmation meant much more to me than all the support from anyone else, so I left my name on the ballot.

Eleanor's stay at the hospital would become brutal. For the first two months, she was in a private room because of the risk of spreading the shingles virus. Her wounds were external as well as internal, with blisters oozing from infected areas. It was hard to watch, but much more painful for her to endure. Her medication caused her to be delusional at times, believing hospital staff were changing rooms on her, which up to that point had not occurred. I went to the hospital multiple times a day to sit with her and comfort her. In the meantime, I had my election brochures made up, intending to deliver five hundred door hangers. In the end, I did not deliver a single one.

I was tossed about by tumultuous emotions, crying my heart out to God, asking, "Why? Why now? I have so much to do and so little time." It was hard to see my beloved wife in pain. It just didn't seem fair. During the candidates' debate, I asked if the mayoral candidates could go first. As I was about to go on the platform, my phone rang. It was Eleanor, frantically looking for me and asking that I come to the hospital. It hurt to hear the desperation in her voice. I called our kids and asked if they could quickly go over to the hospital to be with their mom. My segment of the debate was short, and I left the hall before the rest of the councillors spoke. I remember that night as clearly as if it was yesterday. I could not sleep. My emotions were very raw and I didn't know where to turn. Struggling in my soul, I tossed and turned all night, when suddenly a voice spoke in words from Psalm 46:10: "Be still and know that I am God." That's all I needed. My concerns about the election subsided, all the door hangers stayed in my car and I stopped campaigning. Finally, I left Eleanor in God's hands because I could do nothing for her except be by her side.

Well, the election came and went. I was re-elected for my third term with 70 percent voters' approval. The time between the October 26 election and November 17 would be the most difficult in my life. I had the assurance from city staff and council that I should concentrate on looking after Eleanor and they would help out, picking up the slack at the office. That was such a relief, being free to spend family time at the hospital. One day, I got a call from a nurse at the hospital informing me that Eleanor's shingles were no longer contagious as they were healing externally. They needed her room, so she would have to be moved and share a room with another patient. That was devastating for both her and me. I could no longer spend the nights with her, sitting in a chair beside her bed. After they moved her out—under protest from me—the situation went downhill. Since I could no longer stay the night, I asked my kids to spend a bit more time there for the two days I flew to Abbotsford for a Back to the Bible board meeting. Upon my return, I resumed my vigil at her side, morning, noon and night. She was deteriorating quickly. One morning, I arrived at the hospital and found her sprawled on the floor; she'd been trying to get to the bathroom. It felt like the whole world, including the medical staff, had abandoned her. In actual fact, people had been coming to visit and bringing special food items that Eleanor loved, but in the end she could not eat.

One Friday night, she was so excited because the Maranatha Church ladies' trio had come to sing for her. I had wanted to be there but couldn't make it. She said, "It's okay; they're coming back Monday. Make sure you're here." I promised, and I was there just before lunch on Monday to be with her. At that time, I was informed by Eleanor's nurse that I needed to discuss palliative care with her (the nurse), and so we did. At noon, a musician stopped by on his rounds and asked if he could play for us. I am grateful that he did and very grateful I was there before the ladies came to sing ... just the two of us ... holding her hand when she slipped away.

Forty-six years of our sacred union had come to an end. Together we had raised a son and two daughters, all of them married with children. Eleanor had been a loving grandmother. She was there for our seven grandchildren while they were growing from infants into beautiful kids. Throughout the time of grief and mourning that followed, more than anything, I became deeply aware of the brevity of our time on earth and very thankful for our faith in God as a couple. Today I feel confident that one day believing will become seeing and we will meet again.

The months that followed Eleanor's passing seemed like an eternity. The prospect of being alone in the empty house was chilling. It was the last place I wanted to be. What was left now? Was a career important? Money? Position? Then I had an observation, a realization about what I needed to survive. I needed friends. I needed family. And I needed God more than anything.

Who will you lean on when your partner in life is gone?

* * *

I decided to go back to the office and continue life for what it was worth. Eleanor and I had planned on going on a Caribbean cruise earlier in the year, but due to her illness, we had cancelled that cruise. After she passed away, my kids encouraged me to go on my own, telling me it would be good for me to get away. I appreciated their support and took their advice—even so, I found myself on my patio on the cruise ship crying my eyes out, feeling lost in this world.

A Scrappy Little Nobody

Every evening we had a session with Dr. John Neufeld, along with Phil Callaway in his designated role of trying to be funny. Amanda Stott provided music, which was therapy for my soul. I didn't really want to be with people, but how could I not? After all, this was a cruise ship that held 3,000 guests!

Wanting to be alone, I went late for lunch one day. There was one couple sitting by themselves at a big dining table, so the host asked if I would be willing to join them. Was the host unwilling to mess up another table or was this a providential appointment? I was not sure. But they turned out to be a friendly couple, and as they shared how they met on the internet, I soon became aware of their newly married status. They explained how the dating website they had used allowed users to place parameters around their requirements, guiding the user to the type of individual they wanted to meet. The new husband said he had done all that and somehow the woman he met was not even from his selected search area; he felt it was God who brought them together. He went on to explain that he had taken her up on a cliff to propose to her. While they were climbing, it was drizzling, but when he knelt down on one knee, the sun's rays broke through the clouds and touched them. He felt it was a special blessing from God on their marriage! It seemed he did all the talking, so I asked if they attended a church and what denomination? His wife weighed in then and said that they were looking for a church, but since he was Protestant and she was Catholic, they were struggling a bit.

I replied, "Well, the religion really is not that important, as long as you both have a strong relationship with Jesus."

This took the conversation into another dimension, because she was not sure what I meant. I explained that we all needed forgiveness of sin and Jesus died on the cross to pay for our sins. I showed them a Gideon Bible app that had many answers if they had more questions. She was going to download it as soon as they had internet access. I had heard that before, and honestly, my faith was fairly weak at that moment. Was this a brush-off or was she really interested? The following day, I saw them again. This time she had a pen and again asked me for the name of the New Life app.

The Scripture in this modern era is as close as an iPhone, and the New Life App is available in everyone's preferred translation. It felt good to be able to be of some value, and God confirmed that to me on the cruise. God also opened my eyes to the possibility of another, yet-to-be-written chapter in my life, and He had that one all worked out, I didn't need to worry. The same God that brought me through difficult times in the past was still there to lead me forward into the next phase.

TWENTY-FOUR:
Life's New Experiences

Little did I know how quickly life could change again, though it felt like 2014 had already done a number on me, how could I rebuild? How would I fit in? What would become of my friends, and how could I even be effective in my roles as a family member, church volunteer, community leader and business entrepreneur without a partner?

My experience on the cruise gave me a chance to readjust my thought process, and my conversation on the ship began a new stage of healing. However, there would be challenges. There was a couple on the cruise who decided that I should actually speak to one of the single widows who was with us on the ship; he thought we would be a great match. On our last day, early in the morning before we disembarked, I sat by myself having breakfast and two single sisters were sitting at another table by themselves. I am not sure if the older sister also had matchmaking in mind, but the interchange sure took that angle. I had decided that when we left the ship in Fort Lauderdale, as we had some free time, I wanted to go see the Kennedy Space Center. Well, the sisters decided to join me and we had a brief time to get acquainted, which led to e-contact for a month or so after we all got home. Just friends, of course, and the differences between us meant a relationship simply would not work. She was from British Columbia where her kids were; I was from Winkler and my kids were here. This was not meant to be. I remembered the newly married couple I met on the cruise ship, and I thought, why not follow the path they took?

When I got home, it was close to Easter and my daughter and son-in-law's parents asked if I wanted to join them for a meal on Good Friday. I was ecstatic to finally be invited out and accepted their invitation. Kerry Friesen, a brother to Steve, my son-in-law, was also there. Kerry had just come back from California with a car that Bert Appelt from Appelt Jewelry had asked him to drive back to Canada. He showed me some pictures and said, "This would look good in your garage." It was a beautiful 2007 two-door silver Mercedes convertible! I liked cars and this one renewed the youth in me, even at sixty-six years! By the time it was cleared for import at Walhalla, a week had passed; Bert brought the car to the office at city hall, and yes, the next day the car came home to stay!

I felt very nervous thinking about going onto an online dating site. I did not want others to know I was doing it. I also didn't know how to create a profile and a wish list while being a mayor and still hoping no one would find out. I described myself accurately and, trying to avoid traffic, signed off as Mr. Unrau (my mom's maiden name). Perhaps that would be less obvious. Well, it didn't fool people for long, but it did work for a bit! I had signed up with Christian Mingle, thinking that would narrow the search to a group I could identify with. Well, surprise, surprise! There were many profiles that indicated they were "Christian" in their opinion, by association, but lacked what I thought was the most important part of my search. I looked for a testimony that I could identify with and came across one that struck a chord. It was one that I had glossed over a few times but had bypassed since I was not interested in considering a divorcee, and believe me, that eliminated 95 percent of the options. That was the sole reason why I had dismissed this particular profile earlier. Other than that, I thought her story was genuine, and her faith was alive and real.

One day, I simply clicked "like" on her profile, which meant that "Valerie" would see my profile and could decide whether or not to communicate. It didn't take long. Her response was unexpected—she connected just at a moment when I was busy. She asked if I wanted to chat and I simply responded, "later." Well, that left her with the idea I might not be interested. In fact, I was minding my manners and didn't want to burn any bridges! I did indeed get back to her online; we chatted just a bit and found out quickly where each other lived. She suggested that the best way to get acquainted would likely be if we met in person—she was willing to come from Winnipeg to the Winkler Co-op for supper. I immediately responded, "NO!" My kids had no idea that I was entertaining a new relationship, nor were they ready for that to happen!

Valerie had not been to Winkler for many years, and in her mind, the Co-op restaurant was in the Crocus Mall. I would have gone to the Outpost Grill, the new location at the Co-op Gas station. If we'd gone with this plan, our lives might have ended up going in another direction, with both of us thinking we were stood up! As it happened, I suggested we meet in Winnipeg at The Keg Steakhouse that Saturday night. She agreed. It felt pretty much like I was sneaking around, when normally, I was a pretty open book. Now was the time to take my Mercedes on a dating excursion. The lady seemed very nice, so the gentleman bought her a pretty bouquet of flowers, ordered a private table and planned to arrive at the restaurant early to get everything all set up!

On arrival, I spoke with the hostess, gave her the bouquet and stepped outside to meet this lady, Valerie. I joined a long line of people waiting to get into the restaurant when, from a distance, I saw someone that looked sort of like the profile picture I had seen. She stepped up onto the curb and I greeted her. I introduced myself with my real name and she told me hers. I was looking forward to a nice quiet dining experience, when a Winkler real estate agent, Sandra Banman (also my former employee at Cargill), came up to me and started chatting.

Of course, she had no idea what she was stepping into, but I was getting increasingly uncomfortable. I had come there to meet Valerie for the first time and here she was, silently standing next to me! I stopped our conversation and said, "Sandra, I should tell you, I just met this lady moments ago and we are having dinner here tonight." I must have floored her and she apologized profusely for interrupting. Little did she know how that experience broke the ice for Valerie and me! We laughed it off, entered the Keg and sat down at our "private table for two" with flowers in place.

Glancing at the table next to us, I recognized a large group of people from Winkler, the Fillion family. I knew the family personally, including their daughter Yvette Krahn, who was in the Winkler real estate business, in addition to having been my son's escort at his graduation! They were celebrating Jean's birthday. Valerie recognized some family members from the Alliance Church in Morden. This "private date with Valerie" had just become a Winkler celebration. Plus, now not one, but two local real estate salespeople knew I had dated a lady.

The connections Valerie and I shared extended into the Winnipeg accounting office of Frostiak and Leslie where Valerie was employed. They already knew who I was because Jess Leung, an accountant there, also worked with Yvette Krahn and Sandra Banman at a real estate office in Winkler. Jess had shown Valerie my City of Winkler picture online and told her

I was not Mr. Unrau; I was in fact Martin Harder, the Mayor of Winkler! Now all our cards lay exposed on the table and my secret was out. This was a definite win or lose situation. There was no time to waste in telling my kids that I had met this lady and she was pretty nice! That would be my number 1 job first thing Sunday morning, before they could hear it on the street. The phone was hot and the kids were shocked, not quite ready for what I was telling them.

* * *

So, our first introduction was April 29 online, our first meeting was on May 2 at the Keg and I would introduce Valerie to my kids on May 4. Since I was still hoping to keep this private in the family, I asked Valerie to come as a tourist to Bethel Heritage Park and park her car in a public parking space. Since she drove a red Nissan Juke, which would be as eye-catching at my home as the show window of any car dealer in Winkler, we decided she could not park it in my driveway just yet. As a mayor who was proud of our community, I often did tours for people at the Bethel Heritage Park, so this would be just another "walk in the park." I informed my kids, who lived in Winkler, we would be there at 2:00 in the afternoon and, if they wanted to meet her, to be there; if not, well, it was their choice. But they met her. I didn't sense any solid "No" from Valerie, so we carried on our relationship on a very regular basis. We seemed to have so much in common, including her memory of going to the same church as my oldest sister's family years back.

Valerie was a traveller. Later in June, she travelled to New York City with her friend while I attended a Back to the Bible board meeting in BC. I realized by then that she was a very serious contender for my affection and I felt God call me to pursue the relationship as a possible marriage option, so I bought a few little souvenir items for her. She, on the other hand, bought me a very unique Projects watch, which her girlfriend thought very presumptuous for someone she had just met a month ago online! We had a great summer, and we were pretty sure wedding plans were in our future. I became a bit of a Facebook pro, posting a picture of my new "friend" and immediately receiving a note from a Meryl Matchullis, who introduced herself as my cousin and asked me to "Say hi to Valerie." They had been in youth group together years earlier. On top of that, Valerie's brother, Ron, had sold me my first new Honda Accord at Southland Honda in 1985. Already, it seemed that we were almost family!

In July, just before Valerie's birthday, I purchased an engagement ring. In the parking lot of Church of the Rock in Winnipeg, I asked her, on one knee, if she would accept this ring with the intent to marry me. I thought, "At my age, why wait?" I had pledged to be my first wife's partner for as long as we both lived. I felt that commitment was fulfilled and I needed to look ahead. One day as I drove down the highway, I noticed a sign I had missed earlier. I looked in my rear-view mirror to catch the other side and read: "Why are you looking in the rear-view mirror? You are not going that direction!" I was convinced that God had brought us together.

Valerie felt divorce had left her on the curb and I realized that she hated divorce, as God does. But just because man dumps us beside the highway, does not mean that God leaves us there. Still, the kids in both of our families struggled with their parent getting remarried, and it caused hurt on both sides. One day, I chatted with a friend from the Pilot Mound area, who reassured me. He had gone through a similar situation, but after a year it was all good and married life had become what it was intended to be.

I had booked another trip to Israel, this time with Dr. John Neufeld. I had two options: single room occupancy or share a room with another gentleman and save a few hundred bucks. I informed the tour organizers that before I would agree to share a room, I wanted to have a conversation with the man who would be sharing it with me. He came from BC, and after listening to him describe his use of a machine to help his sleep apnea, I was convinced I needed my own room. I asked Valerie if she would be interested in going. Even though she would be booking her own room, she could at least be on the tour bus with me. She gave it some thought and said it wouldn't work. I left it at that until August, when she informed me that she'd been given a ten-year bonus award from her company and had booked the trip! She did arrange to share a room, but her female roommate snored so loud that the walls vibrated and she was sorry she didn't pay extra for a private room! We contemplated getting married in Israel with Dr. John doing the officiating, but that became too complicated. Plus, we would have had trouble restoring our family relationships if they were not included in the wedding plans. We enjoyed the trip; however, on the way home, we got the news that my brother Don, who had been dealing with cancer, had passed away. This meant we would change our itinerary and stop over in Toronto on our way home. The family delayed his service for a few days to make sure we could get there in time. We were so thankful we had gone to Niagara Falls earlier and had stopped by to introduce Valerie to Don and his family.

Opportunities to connect are precious and need to be taken seriously—like getting married at sixty-seven years old on the backstretch of life. I felt I had met another life mate and was prepared to take the risk of another permanent step of marriage, regardless of family opinions. As my dad said when he remarried at eighty-two years of age, "It doesn't matter if it is for five months or five years; it's less loneliness, one day at a time." He met his second wife as he was viewing the flooded streets of Winkler in 1992, and there she was, sitting on her front porch, praying ... if only she had a man to help her deal with her flooded basement. Well, there he was, and it turned out that the lady had been a neighbour of his in Lowe Farm some sixty years earlier. It proved to be a great marriage, and I no longer got phone calls at 5:30 a.m. to help Dad look for his TV remote!

Valerie and I attended my home church whenever she came out to Winkler and Church of the Rock when I went to see her in Winnipeg on Saturday nights. Wanting to find a church to which neither one of us was previously attached, we connected with Gospel Mission Church in Winkler and asked Claude Lainie to officiate at the wedding. We were married on a beautiful Valentine's Day, February 14, 2016, at the Days Inn Conference Centre in Winkler, with over two hundred people in attendance. The day started a bit blustery, but by mid-afternoon the sun shone brightly on the freshly fallen snow, creating a beautiful backdrop for some great wedding photos. We chose a verse from Ecclesiastes 4:12 (NKJV) as our wedding text: "Though one may be overpowered by another, two can withstand him. And a threefold cord is not quickly broken." Our relationship began with this dedication; with two of us woven and bound together within the love of God, we would have the best opportunity for a lasting marriage.

In her faithfulness, Valerie is a person much like Eleanor, but she is much more of a socializer. Perhaps illness played a part, but it was not in Eleanor's nature to be an initiator in social settings, whereas Valerie thrives in social interactions. She is the hostess of many events, including family get-togethers. God knew that, without Eleanor, I would need support to carry on as mayor, someone who was an active member of our community. People who knew me decades before have come to me expressing amazement that one person could be so fortunate as to have two beautiful marriages, while some never have one. I simply want to say that, in each of my marriage relationships, there was and is loyalty, romance and attentiveness to keep it alive, with a central focus on serving God and others. For the next two terms as mayor, with Valerie at my side, life would definitely take on a different dynamic.

Martin and Valerie's engagement in July 2015

Life's New Experiences

Martin and Valerie's wedding on February 14,
at Day's Inn Conference Centre

Our wedding pictures at Bethel Heritage Park Feb 14, 2016

A Scrappy Little Nobody

Martin and Valerie in Boerne, Texas, in 2022

TWENTY-FIVE:
Drawing a Line

Entering the political world, even at a municipal level required drawing a line in the sand that I found difficult to delineate, not just for one term as mayor, but for all four terms. Each term had different scenarios and different challenges, but basically very similar issues.

My character type was known for getting things done, and Winkler was known for being last on the list of grant recipients. We didn't have patience for the required political games, so we just got things done. At times, I believe that may have been a detriment over the long haul. However, as the story unfolded, it became clear that we did the right thing because it served our people and surrounding communities very well.

In my first two terms as mayor, we built 1,315 new housing units in the city. Winkler became the fastest-growing community in Manitoba while I was in the mayor's chair. It's worth highlighting the reasons why Winkler grew close to three percent annually, going from the sixth-largest city in Manitoba in 2006 with 9,106 people to becoming the fourth-largest city in 2021, with almost 14,000 people, passing Thompson and Portage la Prairie in size. Immigration played a huge role. Winkler's Adele Dyck, through Star 7 International, became the "immigration lady" for this region; she focused on bringing in newcomers from areas affected by the Berlin Wall destruction and enabled many East German residents to emigrate from former Soviet-held territories. The quality of life in Winkler also factored into its growth. It was a good place to live, it was affordable and it was a safe place to raise a family. As people learned about Winkler, they were drawn to it.

Our provincial political leadership during my first two terms was the New Democratic Party (NDP); however, the Winkler area was represented in the Legislature by a Progressive Conservative (PC) member. So, at city hall, we anticipated being in the back benches. We decided we would simply do the things we needed to do, rather than wait for a government program to support our project. Depending on "government programs" significantly increased the costs of every proposal Winkler put forward to government. Our business community was thriving, and the city continued to purchase and develop industrial land to establish jobs and opportunities, creating a long-term, sustainable community. Care for our seniors was lacking, and having an aging population meant something would need to be done about it. Many concerns awaited our attention.

Our fire hall was not adequate to provide the protection needed for our region, so that became the first major challenge to tackle. We began the design and development stage, hoping for some provincial support to build the facility. After all, all the newer fire hall builds in the Province of Manitoba had received some provincial support. We applied for funding, but in the first year of the NDP government under Premier Greg Selinger, Winkler was not his priority and we were told there was no funding available. That did not deter us. We needed to build it, and build it we did, investing our own money and establishing a long-term agreement with the RM of Stanley to support the operating side. It became a "hot point" when we learned that our request for fire hall funding was turned down, but Dauphin, which had an NDP Member of the Legislative Assembly (MLA), got funding! This appeared to be clear political favouritism rather than a decision based on need and a solution based on community. Undaunted, we obtained long-term financing and established the Southern Emergency Response Committee, putting in a forty-year solution. The region would be well served under this plan.

My biggest government department challenge over the years was definitely with the Department of Highways, also known as Manitoba Infrastructure and Transportation (MIT). I had a bit of history with this department back in 1988, when Albert Driedger was Highways Minister under the PC government. I was at Elm Creek; the minister understood the issue at the time and acted to remove a government inspection scale right at our Cargill driveway! Politics played a huge role, but I realized that there were bureaucrats involved who controlled this department and were entrenched in their mindset. The minister had little impact on these decisions unless he genuinely wanted to become actively involved. The government had the Highway Traffic Board (HTB) in place and that was the biggest joke, in my opinion. My problems continued with that department because I challenged their decisions. They seemed to lack common sense, while I had looked at the actual need from the community perspective. In addition, at least a half dozen times, I appeared before the HTB and asked for a lowering of speed zones in our community. We wanted to reduce speed on 15th Street in Winkler, Highway 14 through Winkler, Highway 428 north of Winkler, a road closing north of Northlands Parkway in Winkler, and just within the RM of Stanley north on 428 past Rosebrook Place. All of these situations unfortunately created further conflict between MIT and the City of Winkler.

A Scrappy Little Nobody

The common answer from the government in regard to needed speed reductions was always: "We have done a traffic study and the average speed is … so we determined people are comfortable driving that speed." I had recently acquired a 2007 Mercedes, and I admit I had a bit of a heavy foot. So, I told them about my recent purchase and how it felt pretty good and comfortable at around 160 kilometres per hour. Would that be an acceptable speed? Well, needless to say they were not amused! I persisted in attempting to reduce the speed limits on Highway 14 through Winkler.

At that time, there were two traffic lights, one on Main and the other at the junction between Highway 32 and Highway 14. MIT had placed a crosswalk at the Main Street intersection; however, it was difficult to walk across Highway 14 to Walmart. After several attempts to reduce the speed limit down from 80 kilometres per hour to 60 kilometres and being denied again and again, there was a police report of a "near miss" where a young person was grazed by a vehicle going through that intersection. Ron Lemieux was the minister at the time. I called him to express my outrage and inform him that I, as the Mayor of Winkler, did not want the blood of my citizens on my hands because of these delays in making changes. His answer blew me apart. He said, and I quote, "Martin you can't allow these things to bother you and take those responsibilities personally." That was the final straw! I could no longer depend on that department or minister to make good decisions.

Ministers changed frequently, and it became Minister Steve Ashton's turn to head up MIT. When I approached him regarding the speed limit on Highways 14 and 32, nothing changed. On another visit to the HTB, I again made my case. The engineer for MIT was the "expert" presenter on Highways' position; building the Northlands Parkway School was in discussions and I added that fact to my presentation. The chair of the board asked the engineer, "If the school was already in place, would that change your mind?" His answer was a flat, "No." Another futile effort made, but I was not done.

In 2013, when the Northlands Parkway Collegiate was being built, plans were underway to ensure that the temporary speed limit past the school at 50 kilometres per hour during construction would remain permanent, so again I presented that to the HTB. No movement. Construction continued and plans were made for a permanent crosswalk to be installed. Once more, it was bogged down in bureaucracy and nothing was done. On October 4, communication between the Manitoba Highways Department and me continued, and I received an email from the department saying that there would be no crosswalk installed at that time.

At 3:30 that afternoon, our worst nightmare happened. A student, Carina Denisenko, was walking across Highway 428 outside Northlands Parkway Collegiate—in the place designated for a crosswalk—where she was hit and fatally injured by a northbound vehicle. With the speed limit still at 50 kilometres per hour, it was not the driver's fault. However, if there had been overhead crosswalk lights and signage, surely this fatality need not have happened! The travesty of the story, however, was Minister Ashton, who was in Northern Manitoba at the time, appearing on TV stating that the reason the crosswalk was not there was due to the city not having the drawings for it done. I checked the drawings, and clearly, they were completed. I was interviewed by all major and local media and showed one of them an email from Highways only a few hours earlier that totally negated any suggestion that the city was unprepared. It was the MIT department that said, "No"—I needed to make that clear, as I believe this is what contributed to the long-standing issues I had with the department. I believe I represented the people of Winkler fairly and responsibly, and

I became very disillusioned with the political and bureaucratic posturing I was obligated to take part in.

* * *

Another major long-term venture I thought would never end was the proposal to have the province make Highway 32 a four-lane thoroughfare through Winkler. Earlier, under the previous mayor and council's administration, traffic studies had been done. Those counts were shown in the Department of Highways' own data and indicated, even back then, that Highway 32 was due to be upgraded. How it was resolved was quite the story.

In 2011, the local constituency elected a new MLA and I thought things might change; after all, we were of the same political stripe. I thought I knew him well and he was in my corner. The previous years, when he served in opposition, he faithfully supported my drive to improve and make Highway 32 into a four-lane highway. He was adamant that the City of Winkler should not need to "partner" on this project as a way of expediting it. It was the responsibility of the province to fix their own roads, not the city's job to fix Highways' roads. I assumed that when the Conservatives under Pallister formed government in 2016, with a fortuitous change in provincial cabinet postings, this problem would disappear and we would get Highway 32 done within the first two years of a Conservative government in office. Even with considerable pressure on the government, it took another four years to see any action from the Conservatives, which was the announcement of the construction project.

In the meantime, the City of Winkler had prepared and participated to the tune of over a million dollars to relocate the water and sewer in preparation for the Highway 32 project and had completed all the initial engineering work. By the time the official announcement would be made, broken promises and bottled communication would have come to weigh heavily on personal political relationships. It therefore registered as deeply insulting when the Minister of Infrastructure and the Minister of Finance came unannounced to Winkler, with no opportunity for the City of Winkler to participate in their official announcement about Highway 32. (I was told there would be other opportunities to do more announcements about the highway and I would be invited to take part at that time.) The whole city would have been ecstatic to celebrate this long-awaited news.

Credit for initially putting this project forward was given by the government to the former mayor, who had served fourteen years before. But remarkably, not a word was said about the fourteen years since then! The city was not acknowledged, not even mentioned, nor was the fact that our engineering department did all the grunt work on the design because the MIT had no time! Being left out from any announcements may well have been initiated by MIT staff due to previous run ins; however, I would have thought our MLA would have valued his relationship with his constituents more highly than his political posturing.

Many people called me after the announcement about Highway 32 was made, seeing through the political strategies and recognizing the many years, the multiple hours and the energy we had invested in this project. It would be pretty safe to say the costs were likely triple what they might have been if the job had been done when the need was initially demonstrated. It was no surprise that, in the aftermath of these proceedings, following the tragic loss of a young life, political relationships were soured and continued in a downward spiral to the point where I actually entertained the idea of simply running as an independent provincial candidate.

*　*　*

As it happened, construction was nearing the finish line when my wife, Valerie, and I were invited to drive down that long-awaited road. We happened to be driving east on Roblin Boulevard when, right in front of us, construction workers removed the barricade, opening the road to southbound traffic, and directed us down Highway 32! I felt some measure of vindication and satisfaction for being the first to drive on that new stretch of road.

As time went on, when the Minister of Infrastructure had a falling out with the Conservative party and was sidelined, he approached me to thank me for my determination to represent the City of Winkler in a way that was very rare for any municipal leader. He apologized to me, and we are friends who now have a mutual respect for each other. I saw the value of standing up for the people I represent, not pushing party politics or shoving aside the community I serve and replacing it with self-glorification. These were the real "behind the scenes" struggles I faced as mayor. As I have acknowledged before, I don't do politics well, but I do get things done when politics takes a back seat!

TWENTY-SIX:
Adjustments and Opportunities

Looking back on my courtship and early marriage with Valerie brings back many great memories. After our wedding, we wanted to attend a Johnny Reid concert in Winnipeg. However, when we tried to get tickets, they were sold out. We checked the other places he was performing and found out he would be in Regina! Without a second thought, we decided to go to his Regina concert, take in the Moosejaw Mineral Spa and visit the tunnels as well as the Watrous Hot Springs. It sounded good for a short winter vacation, with an Alaskan cruise planned for a late summer honeymoon. A lot of city responsibilities at that time required my attention, so this seemed the best approach for a limited time away.

Interestingly, I had followed a similar path on my first honeymoon; I had no intentional plan to travel the same route, but it happened! This time around, though, there was definitely the ability to be more elaborate. In our travels, we bumped into a lot of people who I knew but Valerie was meeting for the first time; she lit up every room when she walked in. She was the socializer, and there were a lot of opportunities to mingle as she met her new family and friends.

A Scrappy Little Nobody

In summer, we were asked to represent the Association of Manitoba Municipalities at a municipal event in Ottawa, Ontario. Having served on the AMM board for a while, our executive officer, Joe Masse had gotten to know me fairly well. I was usually outspoken and not afraid to share my thoughts! We went out for dinner one evening and I introduced Valerie to him, knowing him to be a gentleman. Joe had a very funny, dry sense of humour. He looked at Valerie and with a blank expression on his face and said, "Valerie, there may be some things about Martin you don't know. I think he should be a bit more assertive." Valerie appeared puzzled, thinking perhaps she had not met this part of me yet—that certainly was not the man she knew! We had a great laugh, but it was a nice ice breaker.

Initially Valerie knew very few people in political circles; however, being very inquisitive, she enjoyed the dialogue and quickly gained friends. At a Federation of Canadian Municipalities event, while Valerie was in a different part of the building, I happened to be chatting with Winnipeg's former chief of police, Devon Clunis. I asked Devon if I could get a picture with him and sent Valerie a text with the photo. Not to be outdone, wherever she was in the building, Brian Bowman, Mayor of Winnipeg at the time, was close by. So, she introduced herself to him as a former Winnipegger, and with tongue-in-cheek humour, added that she had to marry the Mayor of Winkler in order to meet him. Then she asked for a picture with him and sent it to me by return text. As you can tell, Valerie enjoys a great joke and is not afraid to circulate. We agreed that, whenever I struggled with a name, she would turn to the person I was talking to, introduce herself, and ask, "And your name is?" I felt better. She helped me out with a subtle reminder of the other person's name, and I wasn't embarrassed.

Adjustments and Opportunities

Adjustment in any marriage is a challenge, but I feel ours has gone very well. We created one household out of two and got rid of items that were duplicates. Since my house was oversized for just two people, we had extra space. Guests were always welcome and it didn't matter if they were her friends or mine! Valerie was very considerate. Since the house was only five years old, she agreed to move in and make it a home; it needed her presence and she certainly brought joy back to those rooms. Working together to get a fresh start, we had decided to choose a church where neither of us had attended in the past. In time, we would do the same with a house, but we chose to wait a few years, using the time in the interim to draw ideas on a blank piece of paper, designing our "together forever" home. We agreed that if we disagreed with a concept, colour or layout, we would simply defer to each other on that decision until we both got that *Aha!* moment. It was a wonderful experience and today we are enjoying our new home!

Pretty soon friends from each other's background became mutual friends, and so it was with siblings. While it was not hard to become a "complete family," events with family were generally hosted as smaller separate events rather than combined family events. All the fears and misgivings our kids had about us getting married have disappeared. Valerie is totally involved in Winkler with the Horticultural Society and has served on the executive. Attending municipal events was an opportunity for her to become engaged in my life and to meet many more friends. We are both involved in our church, serving as we can, and we attend a small "life group" as a place to learn and serve others. Annual fishing trips as a combined family have worked well; they are casual enough with no pressure, and everyone looks forward to being together. We had all our kids and grandkids together at an all-inclusive resort in

Puerto Vallarta with very little formal time together, so there was no stress.

I don't do well alone; I learned that quickly. But I can say that, for me, the adjustment to this new marriage has been wonderful. I look forward to many more years and growing old together! I feel that we have been blessed with second chances and my spot in the mayor's chair has been much easier with Valerie at my side. I have three married children, two living in Winkler and one in Texas, and I have seven grandchildren. Valerie has two children, both residing in Winnipeg, and four grandchildren. A multiplied blessing indeed, and great families.

***

Life in the mayor's chair was back on track and having Valerie's support made it much more fun. The 2018 election would be no contest for me as I was once again acclaimed as incumbent mayor. The major work of the new Meridian Exhibition Centre was started, but before the facility was finished, we would encounter COVID-19 and the accompanying challenges. I would finish my term at AMM and concentrate on local issues, which brought much more satisfaction than spinning my wheels on more committees.

The new council this term included the second woman to ever serve on Winkler City Council. When Karina Bueckert was elected, she brought energy and ideas to council that kept the six men on their toes. Yes, she was a firecracker, a great asset to our council, and she served the City of Winkler well. All council members worked hard and in cooperation for the good of community. I found that the many projects completed earlier started paying off as great investments. The community is a very generous, hard-working group from both a business perspective and a caring perspective. The process of convincing

Manitoba Housing to allow us to manage the sixty-six units they owned in Winkler gave me huge personal satisfaction as those homes were being neglected; with no supports in place, the occupants were left to the "wolves," so to speak, and their needs were going unmet.

A community resource officer was hired to assist the police in the community in dealing with minor offenses such as bicycle thefts and parking infractions. This project, in turn, reinforced Central Station to help them build up community resources, including looking after all the affordable housing units in Winkler. From the start, the management for affordable housing units became much better than it was previously, and once we actually transferred title to Winkler Affordable Housing, the situation changed more dramatically. They expanded services created opportunities to walk with the clients, helping them become contributing members of society rather than always being on the receiving end.

We created the Discovery Nature Sanctuary right in the middle of an industrial park, allowing for relief from the stress of a busy workload. Valerie and I found this place to be one of peace and tranquility. It also became a destination for education and relaxation, as well as a space for photographers to hone their skills.

The City of Winkler expended effort to work with the RM of Stanley to formally support the Winkler Stanley Economic Development Corporation with significant funding to develop the immigration initiative for the region and expand the space for the business community to grow. An opportunity came our way to develop an accessible playground with the help of the Canadian Tire Corporation under the Jumpstart program. Winkler was chosen for this venture because of the efforts of David Dunseath, our local Canadian Tire store owner. He called me on a conference call one morning with the vice-president of the foundation as he described the situation. After they finished, he asked if I thought the City of Winkler was interested. Of course, I said, "Yes," and it caught him a bit off guard.

"Do you need to ask council?" he asked. I said, "Yes," but I knew my council and I would commit to a unified yes.

COVID mandates would interrupt the project briefly in the spring of 2020. As it turned out, Canadian Tire Jumpstart Charities programming was also seriously affected. In fact, the operational part was cancelled due to COVID protocols, leaving unused capital funding in place. I presented an idea to council; they were ecstatic with it. We would receive half a million dollars from the sponsoring corporation, the store owner offered another $100,000, which left approximately an additional $125,000 for the City of Winkler to pay. We were back on track to complete the playground project!

As the project took root, an installer was chatting with Rose Toews (who had a grandchild with mobility issues) about building a facility. He referred her to me, as he knew what we were doing. I met with Rose and she informed me that she was thinking of contributing to this project. Her husband, Ryan, had recently passed away and she was wanting to honour him and leave a legacy. I simply stated that, of course, we would offer her a tax receipt for a donation and the amount of money she wanted to contribute was her choice, whether it was a $100,000 or anything less. It was good to see her interest in this cause. As it turned out, she wanted to contribute $100,000! In the end, this left the City of Winkler with a bill of around $25,000 for an almost three quarters of a million-dollar accessible playground. By September 2020, without removing a single established tree, an inclusive Jumpstart Playground was placed in the centre of our main shaded park, a collaborative

Adjustments and Opportunities

project between Canadian Tire Jumpstart Charities, local donors and the City of Winkler.

Another project that took shape during COVID was the outdoor arena in the south end of Winkler at Emerado Park. The surface needed to be paved in order to use it for floor hockey or street hockey. Depressing as things seemed to get during the pandemic era, I thought, "Wouldn't it be nice to get this done during COVID?" It was a $100,000 project and not in the budget. I called five people in the concrete business and, in three days, had enough support to get this project done for less than $25,000. It is invaluable to have that kind of support in this community, and that is what makes this city so successful.

We had a very old dilapidated Golf Course Restaurant and Club House. A group of local golf enthusiasts and business owners decided it needed to be redone. Well, by fall they had raised close to two million in cash, and construction began on this $2.5 million community project. This all took place during a time when the world stood still and didn't know what to do!

In 2013, my family invested $750,000 into bringing Winkler youth a laser tag facility, known as Rush Laser Tag and Entertainment. However, after seven years of not having enough community support and experiencing difficulty getting qualified staff, we were forced to close the doors. It was a huge loss for us and for the community. In January 2020, I was fortunate to get out of the lease, sell off a bit of equipment and close it down. On March 6, the last truck was loaded up with what remained of this venture. March 7, Valerie and I flew to Fort Lauderdale for the weekend. On our return and with the COVID scenario beginning, we were glad we were rid of that operation. Our losses could have been much worse. I concluded that with every loss there is a gain. We just have to look on the bright side. If we had not closed Rush Laser Tag, Valerie and I would not have been able to go on that trip!

For our trip to Fort Lauderdale, we decided we would simply backpack, make no hotel reservations and book a water channel tour with dinner on an island! We exited the plane with minimal belongings on our backs. Cruise dinner tickets in hand, we approached a taxi and asked the driver if he knew where this boat dock was. "Yep," he said and delivered us to the dock. Since we arrived a few hours ahead of our departure, we stood looking across the little bay and saw there was a beautiful hotel! We would need two nights, but it was spring break. They were running a marathon and all the hotels were full.

I told the hotel clerk our story: we had only come for dinner and an extra day, we had made no reservations, but we wondered if by chance they had any room.

She laughed and laughed at our funny story and confirmed, "Sir, for you guys, I have one king room overlooking the ocean."

We had dinner and the next day just went for walks along the beach, enjoying our time. Being spontaneous in embarking on this adventure and yet serene in working out that experience resulted in the greatest joy we could have expected! There would certainly be more unexpected moments to come, but God knew what was ahead. Once again, we felt He looked after us to give us that final break. Just before the COVID storm would hit!

TWENTY-SEVEN:
A Voice in the Wilderness

One day in my second term of office, my staff and I we were sitting in the coffee room at city hall. Yes, I took time for "coffee" with the staff; I must say that their company kept me focused on whom I was serving and who the people were in the background making me look good! Many times, I enjoyed picking up goodies at the nearby bakery to share at coffee time as a treat for staff. Thank you to all the city staff who participated in those coffee times throughout the years!

On one particular break, we were having some fun with a Low German slang term, *Oba yo!* For those unfortunate readers who do not understand this hilarious, unwritten language, it simply means "Oh, yes," or "For sure, yes." Well, to emphasize the positive, both for staff as well as the public, by the end of this bantering coffee break, we had decided on a new Winkler slogan, "Yes Winkler!"

Approaching any project with an attitude of "Yes" makes a huge difference in the outcome. I had experienced that with the many enterprises that have been a part of my life. Now "Yes" became ingrained in our employee culture as well as any public promotions, including the logo change to "Yes Winkler!" Whenever new plans were presented, the approach was "Yes, as long as we take into account, or as long as we look at …" It continued to be the way we considered a proposal or looked at any commercial, industrial or residential development. I believe this really set the stage for the programs we would embark on and clearly made the difference whether a project was doable or not.

In the fall of 2016, two bright, energetic individuals came to Winkler City Hall to discuss an idea that would identify Winkler as the hub and community leader in the amplification of high-speed internet by providing access to every home and business in the city. We listened. We looked at the proposal. We saw the excitement in the face of the "brain child," Hank Wall, and concluded this idea was worth pursuing and making a reality.

For years, I had been in contact with Bell MTS, asking for the expansion of high-speed internet and the answer was always that "Winkler didn't warrant the investment because there was not enough volume." On this day, when we saw two people with an idea and a vision to make this happen, it was exciting off the bat! Now the issue was how would we do this, how could we as a city support them and give their creation a kick-start?

After city hall was presented with the high-speed internet invention, which was enticing, we looked at their ask, and yes, we felt we needed to invest in the project. How secure was the investment and how positive were we that this would be successful? When we received those answers and were assured that all our city line loop would remain ours, regardless of the company's success or failure, it made the decision to contribute half a million dollars a fairly solid investment. Then, choosing a high-profile location for the company to build on and selling them that property for one dollar along with a solid plan for the company to repay the purchase value amount from annual internet hookup fees, our concerns were cleared and the investment secured. This is why the company chose Winkler as the place to do business: because we saw their vision and gave them the go-ahead to reach their dreams too. Saying "Yes Winkler!" to this high-profile venture from a local boy made this decision easy for the city.

Without Winkler's willingness to give this internet company their start, they would never have been able to get financing or appeal to other shareholders for backing. Without that support, they would never have been able to go to the Province of Manitoba to attain favourable investment tax credit status to attract further backing. Having achieved success in Winkler, without further lenders, they would never have been approved for federal high-speed internet funds, an initial $10 million for expansion. They would never have tempted a huge European investment fund to invest hundreds of millions, only to be matched by federal infrastructure funding to literally explode the installation of individual fibre direct internet serving the entire Province of Manitoba, with a focus on filling a desperate need for service to rural Manitobans. This company had previously been in discussions with neighbouring communities that were either not willing or not able to say "Yes" to this project. Perhaps they simply didn't catch the dream or have the foresight to support them.

I am thankful that we hatched the *Oba yo!* or "Yes Winkler!" slogan around a coffee table, generating a beneficial project that has now had a huge impact for all previously under-serviced internet users that the huge corporate world had previously ignored!

Never lose sight of a dream, ensure it is well researched, make sure it meets a need and go for it!

Why was this such a big deal? Because today we have shown the world what can be done with an idea; it's no different than the outcome of a council meeting where a young soccer team brought us the first installment of twenty dollars for the now very well-functioning $22 million-dollar Meridian Exhibition Centre that would also highlight the power of "Yes Winkler!"

* * *

Winkler was built on the bald prairies with little to no long-term water runoff. This resulted in the installation of deep wells into the Winkler Aquifer to provide the majority of Winkler's water supply. In my first term of office, we signed an agreement with the Pembina Valley Water Cooperative (PVWC), at the time under the management of Sam Schellenberg, to purchase 40 percent of the Winkler water supply, which in turn meant that the entire region could actually borrow the money to build a facility to supply water from the Red River to this region. Being a regional player was important and it seemed only appropriate. However, Winkler's success added much stress to my term as mayor from smaller, and I will say competing, communities. There were many times I just swallowed hard and moved on.

As a city, we had feverishly tried to get an increase in our drawing capacity from this aquifer and were denied many times simply because the Manitoba Water Services Board felt it could do significant damage to our future water supply from the aquifer. Protecting the aquifer was drilled into our minds, and we always had that uppermost in our decision-making process. During my first term in office, we continued to look for alternative water supplies for Winkler. Our city engineer, Johan Botha, was very determined to apply for increases to our aquifer source of water. Eventually he decided we would put in a request for increased water supply, promising to withdraw the brackish water (somewhat like sea water that can't be used for household needs) from the level below our wells. This would not contaminate the aquifer but would, in fact, ensure the brackish water would not push up and penetrate the fresh water source. We worked together with Winkler Bible Camp at the time, when they established their "beach" and filled it with brackish water. It worked so well; the brackish water actually became fresher as it was pumped. So, we received a per year increase to double our extraction of brackish water.

In 2012, our new water treatment plant was opened (also referred to as a reverse osmosis drinking water plant or R/O), funded with a tri-party agreement with the feds, the province and Winkler. This made life much easier as we continued to grow rapidly. With the Manco/Saputo dairy plant in Winkler closing, we had additional water supply and sewer capacity for years to come. We had achieved a definite win-win situation for us, as well as for the region.

Then in 2021, we faced a drought. The PVWC, especially their processing capacity, ran low in supply. Morden, in particular, was in dire straits. Lake Minnewasta was dangerously close to running dry. The entire region buckled down to come up with a sustainable solution. As the City of Winkler, we pitched in, using our R/O system to capacity and reducing our formal agreement for supply from PVWC. We simply picked up our portion in the slow time in winter, wanting to be a part of the regional solution. The PVWC expanded the waterline capacity to deliver more water to Morden, though the city thought at the time that they didn't need and would never need the PVWC. They felt it would be an unnecessary burden to carry; after all, they had the lake that never ran dry. Initially, they did install a very small line to deliver five percent of their water needs. However, in 2021, Morden increased its capacity from PVWC.

The "lake that never ran dry" is of very integral value to replenishing the Winkler aquifer in the spring. In fact, in the summer of 2021, when aquifer levels were dropping, there was a noticeable increase when Morden's lagoons were released. That may not sound too appealing, but it's really no issue. It's a natural cleansing process as water is absorbed into the aquifer and used again—no different than any other urban centre, including the PVWC using Red River water to serve the entire region. So, as we would say, "what goes around, comes around" as we recycle a very life-giving source: our own drinking water. This does mean we are a region depending on each other for survival and no project can stand on its own.

The drought of 2021 provoked a particularly unsettling political irritant between our local constituency MLA and me. Our engineer, Scott Toews, had what we thought was a brilliant idea to reduce future dependency and add stability to our combined water supply. We asked for increased capacity to be built at our Winkler plant, which on occasion could push water into whatever direction was needed. We had already done that on occasion, when Boundary Trails Health Centre or the rural municipality was struggling to receive sufficient water through the co-op. We were willing to do that.

When our provincial politicians made their trek to the Red River and Lake Minnewasta to determine ways to supply Morden with water, they created a photo op of their presence at the location of the crisis, making a brief stop, and included the Winkler R/O plant on their route. To this day, our request to bring the capacity of the R/O plant in Winkler to its full potential as a regional water supply has been entirely ignored. The elected officials did not appear to be there to listen to solutions. Instead, their plane was booked for a "fly over" to determine how they could bring water from the Patterson Pits, our Winkler main aquifer recharge, and pump that water directly into Lake Minnewasta to supply Morden.

They fully ignored the sensitive environmental recharge spot, a small gravel pit, and exposed that water to a bigger body of water with a much higher evaporation rate. Our engineers informed us that robbing our recharge at Patterson Pits could, in fact, totally ruin the aquifer stability we had tried to protect—and that's where the wheels on the little red wagon fell off. Clearly, this was a time when "Yes!" was the wrong reply. When I called the Minister of Finance to simply say "No!" (as in *Oba Nay!*), he, of all people, told me to "stay in my lane!" To which I replied, "If something that could impact the future water supply for the City of Winkler forever is NOT my business, I have no lane at all!"

Aquifer research and the potential risk of damaging the aquifer had not been taken into consideration by the province. This was simply unacceptable to us and appeared to be a completely political move by the province based on position, not on knowledge of what was at stake. In the fall of 2021, it was noted that, because Winkler was growing so fast, the PVWC could not fully supply the smaller, totally dependent users. This was the time we looked at our water usage records from the PVWC and confirmed that, not only had Winkler never exceeded the total initial volume we had taken fourteen years earlier, the city had grown from just over 9,000 people to almost 14,000. The City of Winkler has always found ways to be self-sufficient and responsible in growth. While Winkler may always evoke friendly rivalry with other communities, this city will continue to exemplify leadership while striving to be good neighbours.

TWENTY-EIGHT:
Seeing through the Clouds

What could happen if you ignored politics and put the combined efforts of a community into one project? We saw what happened with Bethel Park, we saw what happened with the fire hall, and we saw what happened when we worked with industrial and commercial ventures, putting the tools in place for them to thrive. That is the story of Winkler! We had developed a program where the municipal tax portion for any commercial or industrial expansion with a new build was phased in over six years. People appreciated the gesture, and even though not every business' success may have depended on it, it became another reason to celebrate Winkler. Our community business world is primarily made up of self-made success stories that began in a back garage, perhaps as a mom-and-pop shop that became a 1,000-employee business, like Triple E and Lode King. Triple E Developments spun off into the next generation and continues to facilitate developmental expansion in Winkler. The vision of one or two people became a huge part of Winkler's success.

City of Winkler amenities could not have included a full eighteen-hole golf course and a new club house without our business community. The Pine Ridge Skate Park and Winkler Beach Volleyball as well as the two basketball courts adjacent to the skate park were all funded by individuals and businesses working together. The addition of Arctic Field, a new ballpark, was another business investment partnering with the city, but we were not the lead. (Being recognized and getting the credit was not important; meeting the need and getting the job done was our highest priority. This is something all our politicians need in their inauguration portfolio. Every council needs to make this an oath of office: "Others before me, community before self-ambitions.") Businesses like Steel Tech or Icon Technologies Limited would not be established in Winkler had we not worked together to make it happen. The Clover Creek Learning Centre for Autism Spectrum Disorder would not be here without the generosity of John Loewen from Icon, whose sole support met a need in the wider community, including his own grandson who was diagnosed with ASD.

Early in my role as mayor, one such personal need was made known to me by Peter Krahn, owner of the Bible Book Shop. His wife had been diagnosed with cancer. After a lifetime of contributing to the success and future of Winkler, he was unable to retire here because we did not have the amenities and supports needed to age in place. Peter Krahn's plight prompted the idea of beginning a project for seniors with food service and light housekeeping. Walter and Linda Siemens came on the team with me to work on this project. (This really was not a city project, but I happened to be the mayor working on an outside committee on a project of greatest need. These meetings were never on the city's expense list of meetings for which I was being paid.) We hired Larry Penner from Calgary as project leader and the work began in earnest. This facility was to be a full-service seniors housing unit, with the official participation of the existing seniors centre. The nine-storey building would house the Winkler Seniors Centre on the main floor, with supportive housing for residents with higher needs on the second floor. I had a great comrade in Carolyn Ryan, who worked for Manitoba Housing. She was a great support, and I truly believe that, without her, we never would have received the $60,000 per unit support for forty-eight designated affordable suites, twelve on each remaining floor from the third floor up to the ninth, with another twenty-four-premium full-retail independent units, two per floor. After Carolyn left, we were unsuccessful in getting supportive housing funding for the second floor.

The Buhler Active Living Centre was eight years in the making from beginning to occupation. Many hurdles, many naysayers, including Winkler Seniors Centre, who owned the property and wanted ownership of a portion of the building. We had determined this to be impossible in view of our financing challenges. Once the design and estimates were done, we understood that perhaps we had bitten off a bit more than we could chew!

Approximately a million dollars was raised in donations, but the project came in at a cost of 28 million! Not quite enough to cash-flow this! Not to be deterred, we attained a grant of $2.88 million from the province for the forty-eight affordable units plus the additional twenty-four full-rent end units. These would all be life lease, with $60,000, $80,000 and $100,000 deposits to be repaid upon vacating the unit. It all made sense as we went out with proposals requesting financing for this project. The local credit union began by asking us for a 60 percent occupancy commitment before we started building. When we got to that point, they had decided on 80 percent occupancy and they would float the construction period by requiring interest-only payments and then converting it into a mortgage. The challenge became, how do you sell eighty-year-old people (or anyone) on a concept when there is good reason to believe that by the time it is built, they may not be alive anymore? On top of this, government rules were such that deposits needed to be placed in trust and could not be used for construction. With all these requirements, it seemed impossible, but we carried on. We approached our business community to see if they would "buy" the units upfront. Then, once the project was completed and we had actual residents' deposits, the businesses would carry their portion as a community support endeavour.

The culmination of all our hard work, or you could say, "the icing on the cake," came as I was sitting in my office thinking about a great philanthropist, Johnny Buhler. I had the idea that I should call his foundation and see if there would be any interest in naming rights. I was surprised when Johnny actually answered the call himself! I explained who I was and what the project was. He immediately told me about all his bad experiences in the area and why this region would never get another single cent. After allowing him to unload for a bit, I asked if he had ever done any project with me and of course he had not. He asked me to send him the information. This was a Thursday afternoon. I made sure to include the drawings, complete with his name on the building to indicate how it could appear, and personally delivered the proposal to the post office by Friday noon to ensure it would be out on the first available mail route delivered by registered mail. This was the long weekend in May.

On Tuesday morning as I arrived at the office, my phone rang; it was Johnny and Bonnie. They were intrigued with what we were trying to accomplish, and although he had not yet received the package, they wanted to come that afternoon. I called up Walter to tell him the story and he wrote up a preliminary agreement for naming rights. We would ask for $1.25 million, and if we were successful, we could start the project immediately. When they walked into my office, I was shocked to see Johnny with the package in hand! The "ask" was made and discussions pursued, followed by a tour of the location. By 4:00 p.m., he signed the agreement; as Johnny mentioned at the sod turning later in August, this was the fastest he had ever given away over a million dollars in his life! We were so grateful for their continued generosity over the next five years of construction, making this project a success!

The province never did come through with supportive housing, and for two years the second floor sat empty. Then Silver Lining Care, a private group from Steinbach, working with government home care services for partial support, set up their program, and today the second floor is full—with a waiting list! The facilities came together as planned; the city assisted with a quarter-million-dollar principal support as well as six-year phased-in tax support similar to the business community program. Again, the City of Winkler was not the initiator but, rather, a support mechanism to ease the burden on those providing for this community need. Community support has been tremendous, including the completion of the second-floor outdoor terrace, making this an inviting place for prospective tenants to come to visit. The added services of a pharmacy and hair salon were vital features, and the pending addition of medical care is still an option.

* * *

Another project, also eight years in the making, is the new arena and community sports plex. This project began with a soccer team coming to a city hall council meeting with twenty dollars to their name, wanting it to go towards a future complex. Small steps of action can lead to significant endeavours, and dreams can become a reality! Discussions about partnering with us to build this facility started with the Stanley Agricultural Society, and discourse seemed to be on track but lacking a common vision of what could be accomplished. The Ag Society started splitting hairs as to which part was theirs and which parts the City of Winkler could operate. They wanted to establish a base as well as an identity for the Ag Society, and they didn't feel the city was there to help them achieve that. This, in my opinion, was a recipe for disaster, and we began deliberations for the city to simply purchase the property from them. Committee meeting after committee meeting took place until we had established a price that would be presented to the "membership" for consideration.

Community attendance at the sports plex proposal meeting was very sparse. A few members decided to bring friends that didn't like the idea. Although board members were in majority, according to the bylaws, they could not vote, and therefore the offer was defeated. Another controversy arose around the idea that the facility should be a joint Morden/Winkler venture, located in the corridor between the two communities, perhaps close to the Boundary Trails Hospital. The irony of this disagreement was that this plan was considered to be a regional community relationship builder.

I was not in favour of the idea to build the sports plex between Winkler and Morden because I learned that urban sprawl was extremely costly and, in fact, could wreck both the Morden and Winkler nucleuses. The proposed recreational facility could catapult development surrounding it and exact a financial toll from both communities. Since we had no public transportation system in place, the study also determined low viability of citizens walking to the facilities. It was the local students who would benefit most from the proposed complex. Over 2,000 students located in four schools—Northlands Parkway, Parkland Elementary, Garden Valley Collegiate and Winkler Elementary—were all close by.

The facility was projected to be built in three phases: the secondary arena, the soccer pitch and the pool. Although the Ag Society couldn't see the overall vision for this sports and entertainment centre initially, I was able to negotiate the purchase of their property, right in the centre of Winkler, surrounded by ball diamonds, soccer fields, the accessible park and the pool! Sports central! Construction began in earnest just before COVID. Both phase one and phase two, the arena and the soccer pitch, got done at the same time; this included connecting them to the old arena. We are now anticipating renovation of the Centennial Arena, built in 1967, and upgrading that structure in 2024. Phase three, yet to be started, is an indoor pool. As before, no funding has been available from any government source to date.

I pursued another major industry in the city, Meridian Manufacturing Inc., as well as the Edwards Family Charitable Foundation for contributions to naming rights. At my next "state of the city" address to the Chamber, I invited the young man who came to city hall with his twenty bucks to come on stage as we unveiled the $22-million project and to meet the Meridian rep, who delivered a quarter-million-dollar initial payment! It was an object lesson on multiplication and how small dreams can grow and become a reality!

Once again, we received $1.25 million in cash for naming rights for the Meridian Exhibition Centre as well as for the Bernhard Thiessen Hall. Bernie, now retired, was the individual responsible for bringing the Meridian Group to Winkler years earlier, and Meridian Industries and the Edwards family wanted to honour him with this recognition.

* * *

The Meridian Exhibition Centre facility was built during the COVID era. When the coronavirus and government mandates hit with a vengeance, the official scheduled opening was delayed again and again. The community divide over issues raised by the COVID vaccine caused severe backlash, including a period of time when we could only open the facility for those that were vaccinated. The unvaccinated residents claimed a double standard and threatened to withhold taxes because non-vaccinated individuals could not use the facilities. These were tough times, but in forging a common goal, we survived the storm, and now the Meridian Exhibition Centre is a wonderful addition to our community and the region.

Winkler was a very well-managed city with healthy budgets and surpluses that made it possible for us to independently find our own way by fundraising for capital and operating costs. To our advantage, if we had waited on government funding for the Meridian Exhibition Centre, we would still be waiting and the facility costs would now balloon to over $40 million. Today, the funding support would simply disappear in the additional costs involved to construct the facilities.

I have reached a very carefully considered conclusion in my term as mayor: provincial and federal governments have become entities to promote themselves and the next election bid. In contrast, communities and individuals residing in small town municipalities actually make a difference and make decisions because they are the right thing to do to serve their people and deliver the services most people in their community need on a daily basis. It is also very clear that universal program funding simply drives up prices and causes inflation, as everyone needs to buy the same goods and use the same construction firms, creating universal project cost increases.

Martin receiving the Queen's Platinum Jubilee Award for community service

Martin on city council giving his last official signature in 2022, selling another industrial land development

A Scrappy Little Nobody

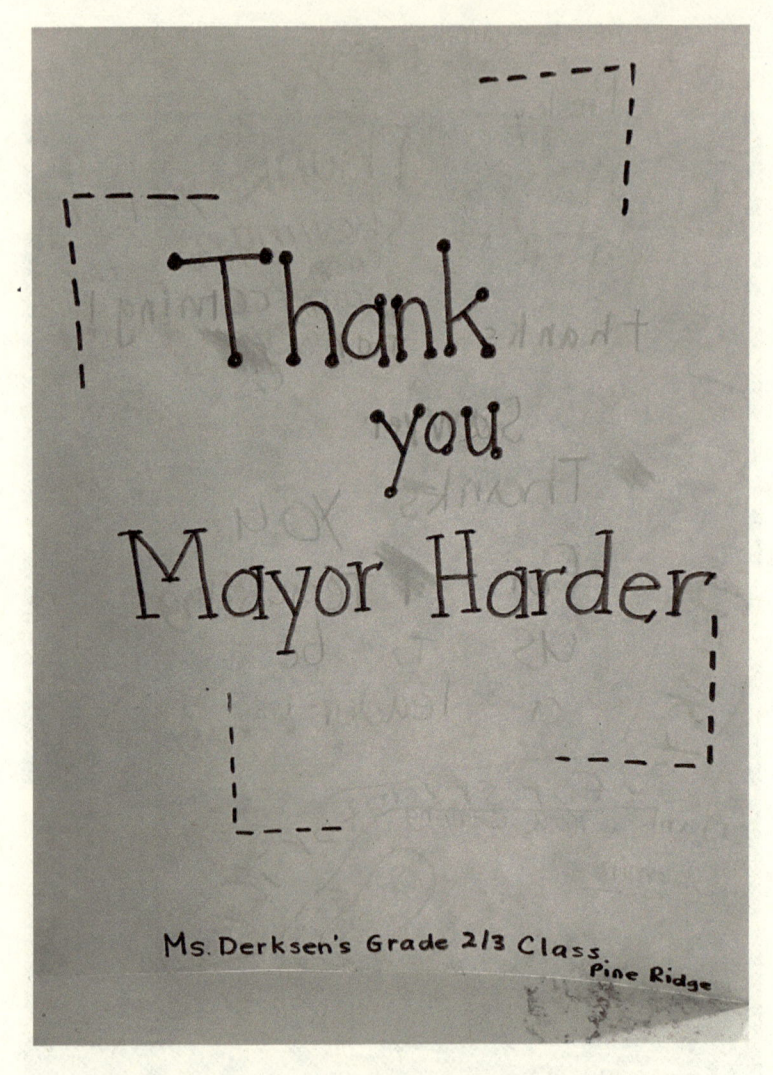

Mayor thank-you from Ms. Derksen's Grade 2/3 class at Pine Ridge Elementary

TWENTY-NINE:
Managing Crisis with Vision for the Future

Two essentials for keeping a community alive and growing are a dependable water source and an environmentally friendly wastewater disposal system. The clean water issue and the wastewater issue are closely tied together. Situated on the flat prairies, Winkler has always had to struggle with water sources. A lack of natural runoff from hills or rivers to dispose of our water results in unique challenges. Nor are there lakes or rivers in which to dump wastewater on a daily basis; therefore, we have the challenge of using the available access to our aquifer. We must store our wastewater until the creeks run in spring, release our treated wastewater into the stream and release it again before fall freeze-up, as ice could accumulate, causing further infrastructure damage by taking out bridges and so on during spring runoff.

Along with receiving authority to treat our water through the R/O system came even more pressure, and it left wastewater disposal as an outstanding issue. The spring of 2010 was exceptionally wet and particularly challenging. Many Winkler homes had ground-drainage issues, and sump pumps were going twenty-four hours a day. Along with other broader area ground seepage, the system was overwhelmed, filling our lagoons faster than normal.

There are two reasons for specified lagoon release dates: water quality, a Manitoba Environmental Department (MED) responsibility, and timing of the release because of low flow in the stream, which tends to build up ice, a Manitoba Infrastructure and Transportation responsibility. Limited lagoon storage capacity and our preapproved release dates set for June and October (due to seasonal excessive use) meant that any deviation from the plan for an early release of wastewater into a low-flowing creek would require approval from both MED and MIT due to their concern for quality of water and potential ice build-up in spring. It was difficult not to raise red flags with MED and MIT. They erroneously attributed our request for early release to ongoing rapid growth and expansion in Winkler's housing and business sectors. As a result, they did not take into consideration that the current scenario was a one-off situation due to excessive runoff issues that year.

While it was true that Winkler was one of the fastest-growing communities in Manitoba, which meant added pressure on our wastewater capacity, this was not the issue at hand. The government needed additional information, and they needed to adapt their expectations and reconsider their permission for early release. This was making water issues more complicated, as the 2010 situation was a one-off event caused by excessive moisture one spring, not because of rapid city growth. But that was what happened. It made the government bureaucracy look good in that they controlled us and our growth, and stopped the building of subdivisions in Winkler for a time.

There had already been numerous discussions on how to handle the wastewater. The challenge that remained was the cost of this venture and the time required to build it. At that time, we had a wet industry in town. Manco milk processing (later sold to Saputo) was a gigantic water user as well as wastewater contributor. It seemed like all the stars were lined up to address the issue—at an inappropriate time. It was one of those moments when all hands should have been on deck to find a solution and come up with a consolidated plan. Instead of having productive conversations about the wastewater release date and the one-off weather-related water runoff situation, MED decided that, until the early sewage release date matter was addressed, there needed to be a stop order on any further development of subdivisions in Winkler. Once that edict came down, as far as subdivisions were concerned, everything ground to a halt. There was no further willingness on the part of government to compromise until a plan was laid out for a wastewater solution. In 2011, I was building a new home and had several lots that I needed to resize. A subdivision became necessary, not to add more load, simply to readjust property lines. By this time, the government bureaucracy had become so complicated that my application was rejected. As a result of this one-time weather event in 2010, our administration and council concentrated on finding a big picture solution. Plans for a mechanical treatment facility were initiated and pursued. A project this size was too much for our community to do on our own; therefore, an application for funding a wastewater plant was activated.

Several changes transpired over the next number of years. Our biggest water user and wastewater producer decided to abandon operations in Winkler and build a new facility in Brandon. That was a blessing in disguise (we discovered). With the absence of this one wet industry, we actually gained 30 percent capacity in our lagoons. Restrictions for subdivisions were removed and growth continued. Although the application process for funding had begun, we never reached the point of approval. We had four different changes in federal political administrations, which meant that, with each new government, the application needed more information or had to start over from the beginning. This process became extremely frustrating; we never did require an additional early release permit, so we carried on. This reminded me again of the importance of continuity in government and the value of multiple-term councils to follow through with any plans.

In 2019, it appeared that our application for funding the wastewater treatment facility was receiving attention and about to be approved. When both provincial and federal grants seemed on the verge of agreement, we pursued the process of preliminary design and class "C" estimates to finalize our plans. Since this needed to be a regional project, we created an application as a region, where Winkler, Stanley and Morden would file under one requisition. We discovered initially that, because Morden was using a separate and different design proposal that did not align with the province's approved process, the project was delayed while waiting for the review and adjustment of their proposal. Meanwhile, our application was put on hold again. Since the Morden case was not approved, once more we carried on with the idea of splitting up the project as phases one, two and three, still under the same application. Finally, we passed that hurdle and went to tender, with approval certain for January 2021.

Mere days before the agreed announcement, the press release was cancelled and we were told the province had a big announcement to make. Well, that proved to be false, and by that time, we were dealing with COVID and didn't know what was up. Finally, we got the answer. The federal government was not happy with our efforts to consult with and get input from the Indigenous and Métis people. We had provided these communities with all the information and mailed the package with the deadline we were given, with no response. Eventually we did have a meeting and found there were no environmental concerns about the application. However, those three months of extra wait time proved to be extremely costly. When the official approval was finally announced on June 21, 2021, inflation had begun to set in.

Although our Winkler/Stanley portion of the wastewater treatment facility application for $48 million was approved, the lowest tender now came in at $65 million—much higher than the original application amount but an attempt to reflect inflationary prices that had occurred in the time lapse between application approval and final tender submissions. That shocked all of us! The province was limited to their 33 percent of the original $48 million price tag, the federal government kicked in 40 percent and the municipal portion was the remaining 27 percent. This overage left an additional $17 million for us to deal with and neither the province nor the feds would contribute toward the additional outstanding balance. This amount was simply too much for any municipality to bear, never mind the future cost of the Morden portion. Their new design requirements made their situation astronomically worse than ours. We knew there would need to be some flexibility in our approach to this project.

Going forward, efforts were made at every level to come to a compromise, but there would be no give. Attempts were made to source other department operating funds. We offered to pick up half of the $17 million on our tax bill if the province would pick up the rest. We tried to get the federal government to participate; after all, they were responsible for delaying the project! They would have none of it.

One day, both our City of Winkler manager and engineer were in Brandon at a water services event where the province would be represented. On their way home, I received a call from our city manager. They had been told there was great news, and he assumed that meant the province would participate.

We were asked to join a conference call with the provincial Minister of Economic Development at 5:30 on a Friday night. We were all excited and got on the call—only to be told there would be no further provincial support. Instead, the province wanted to ask the successful bidder to hold their bid for thirty days. The low bidder refused to extend a bid offer, which meant we needed to pursue the next lowest tender and add another seven million to the overall bid value. We were still willing to split the first overage but felt the extension request was entirely the provincial decision; therefore, that would be their bill. The situation continued to deteriorate. Eventually, the province came up with a proposal to meet with the municipalities of Morden, Stanley and Winkler, adding in the Pembina Valley Water Co-op to propose an entirely different financing option using the federal infrastructure bank.

The provincial proposal was presented to the entire group as one lump-sum project promoted by the economic development officer, our local constituency MLA (several other cabinet ministers were also present) and two officers from the Canada Infrastructure Bank. That meeting went downhill from the opening comments. The new proposal was to unload all of this debt and create a project worth $200 million, with no more government support. We would just borrow the money as municipalities and all our problems would be gone.

The first and obvious question I had was, how can we even borrow this amount? It exceeds our borrowing capacity according to the *Municipal Act*. The answer: this would be a separate corporation and would not end up on our balance sheet. Since we still needed to ensure this loan would be paid off, it was suggested the amount could be spread over thirty or thirty-five years. Well, none of these municipalities had ever borrowed money over thirty years so that was hard to accept. My next question was, how will this be funded? The answer: utility rates. Next question: well, how high would these rates need to be to be able to cover operating and debt payments? The answer to this question literally blew me away: if initially the rates are not enough, we will just add the interest to the principal! *Now I smelled a rat.* If I, as an individual, handled my finances in that fashion, took the credit card bills I could not pay, added them to my mortgage and went deeper into debt, would that work? The light went on! This is what governments have done for years, and that is why this country is in financial trouble. The government is not required to balance their budget. In the municipalities, it doesn't work that way. We are required by law to balance our budgets—as we do as homeowners or business persons—we need to have a strong balance sheet!

How could it be that a room full of ministers of government (including our local MLA) would ever come up with such an absurd proposal? In that moment, I lost respect for the candidates we had elected to look after our best interest. There and then I got up and said, "NO, I will not mortgage my grandchildren's future to accept such a ludicrous proposition." I am so thankful we as an entire region turned it down and sent them packing. The situation now required us to go back to the drawing board and come up with another plan. (However, eventually, subsequent to this event, the province did step up to right the wrong and offered additional support.)

As I reflect on this scenario, I understand why I don't like politics. I had simply tried to represent our community and protect Winkler *from* politics. This is the reason I will never run for provincial or federal office: there seems to be a disconnect between reality and reasonable thinking. My reply to the Minister of Economic Development was that this was another "download" to municipalities that I was not falling for.

I had learned to speak up when what I heard was simply not a realistic or reasonable solution. Again, the government politicians came with their own version of an answer, a resolution, without even asking us if this one made sense for our community. I invented a new word that day, "consultold." That is literally how we were approached, not consulted to see if we could work this out but coming to tell us, to convince us they were our superiors and therefore must have a better solution. I was not there just for another photo op. We needed a workable idea, effective for the future growth and development of this region at a level we could afford.

I learned in life that it is important to understand a situation before jumping to conclusions. I learned the value of speaking up when something doesn't "smell" right. I discovered that political agendas are there for what you can gain from the media rather than what is of value to the community. I am thankful I had a council well versed in financial matters. Together we were looking out for our residents, avoiding a future disaster we simply could not afford.

At this time, my decision not to run for another term had already been made. Still, the threat of a new candidate running as mayor, someone who would completely destroy what we had worked for in the last sixteen years, just seemed overwhelming. In fact, the stress of not being on the ballot in 2022 was greater than it was in any election where I was running. I chose to back my deputy mayor in his decision to run. I supported him and campaigned for him to win. The need for continuity was too important to risk throwing all the years of positive progress away for a one-trick pony.

When all was said and done, the citizens of the City of Winkler elected every incumbent councillor running, one that had served in a previous term and our retired public works foreman. For me, that was satisfaction enough to prove we were on the right track and the community wanted a similar direction in the future. I had served with four city managers and four councils, and we all worked hard together to get the job done.

We now have a great paid on-call fire department and an agreement with the RM of Stanley for regional fire protection. We have a regional waste disposal organization called SWAMP (Solid Waste Area Management Plan). We have a regional planning office, a regional recreation agreement with the RM of Stanley and a regional library. Our police services include a regional tactical team in Altona, Morden and Winkler. A regional water agreement with Pembina Valley Water Co-op serves fourteen different municipalities in our area. And as I write this, we have a joint wastewater project in motion with the RM of Stanley.

THIRTY:
A "Balanced" Approach

The years of COVID illness and government mandates, 2020 to 2022, were considered to be the biggest challenge from any municipal perspective, and it certainly was that for me. There was plenty of press regarding resistance and controversy over COVID-related issues in our region and, to a certain extent, the City of Winkler. The atmosphere was a bit of a Trump-style U.S.A. identification and the anger that developed certainly reflected the Trump era. The good, the bad and the ugly revealed itself, and there seemed to be no middle ground. It didn't help municipalities one bit to have a very domineering premier, whose modus operandi was forcing people to fit his mould and creating tremendous push back. Having a federal prime minister who had no intention of discussing issues or listening to those with differing opinions certainly created justification for protests, regardless if one thought they were right or wrong. However, from a municipal perspective, we were dragged into the controversy, and it did not matter which side of the issue one came from, it was wrong. If one listened to both sides and defended both positions to a point, that was considered cowardice—or even being wishy-washy. One day, an individual was demonized as a lefty, supporting vaccination. Another day, that same individual was

A "Balanced" Approach

considered a hard-right extremist, an anti-health-and-science demon. When I suggested that we needed to listen to our long-term doctors, the ones we had relied on for decades, the strong voices opposed to vaccinations considered me a traitor.

Our world was now living under this scrutiny. Locally, too often neither side understood that the role of municipalities was to function inside Canadian or Manitoba laws according to the *Municipal Act*. Under constitutional and Canadian law, municipalities actually have no legal entitlement other than to serve the wishes of the provincial government, thus the reason for the *Municipal Act*. I firmly believe some of those regulations and structures need to be addressed. As municipalities, we deliver 85 percent of the direct services to our citizens and that needs to be our focus rather than special interest groups or national protests. Believing that municipalities could change this fact in the middle of a health crisis and a political crisis was not feasible. To believe the municipality could ignore the federal or provincial directive was simply ludicrous and, in fact, was not the role of the municipality. Neither could the municipality assume that responsibility.

Communication around the proposal for a "sanctuary city" was respectful, and the motion was given serious deliberation. I challenged each councillor to come up with their own reasons as to why they supported or denied the request, and each one was required to publicly state these reasons. In every case brought before council, we had ample time to determine, based on our understanding, the rationale we used to take a stand on any issue. The notion of transforming the City of Winkler into a sanctuary city simply would not work—besides, for whom and from what were we a supposed sanctuary? From the laws of the land? Or the orders we were subject to from the province?

I didn't think so. If that were possible, this could and would be used or abused to protect any other criminal from being prosecuted for a different offence in a different situation. If we had attempted such a move, we would immediately have been disbanded by the powers held under the provincial government. They would have installed new city management, and our community would have lost all opportunities to make a difference. The role of municipalities or cities is simply to provide basic services to our people, not to some, but to all. That is why compromise and understanding is so vital. In this time frame, the political and municipal responsibilities were confused with federal and provincial laws. People really had no idea where one started and the other left off, including provincial and federal government jurisdictions. When those lines got crossed or mixed up, it only created confusion. Governments at every echelon are smeared because people don't understand the limits of a particular level and how that limitation affects the authority of the lower ranks.

My own position became very clear and I voiced it from the start: I disagreed with the federal and provincial decisions to include mom-and-pop shops in the shutdowns while allowing large corporate stores to remain open for business. I also disagreed with restricting goods purchased to what was deemed essential and non-essential! My essentials are totally different from the next person's. (My brother went into a department store in December—with our local temperatures in the minus 30 Celsius range—looking for a pair of long johns and was told they couldn't sell them because they were non-essential! Well, perhaps they would be on sale in the middle of July!) In response to this decision, I took up a self-funded campaign to "Be Safe, Be Fair, Open Manitoba." This slogan was developed in conjunction with a Steinbach acquaintance who had a sign created that said simply, "Open MB." I felt that was too broad;

A "Balanced" Approach

we decided to be specific and added "Be Safe, Be Fair." This move brought national TV coverage, but unfortunately the government, in this case the Manitoba government, refused to listen. I was outraged that local shops needed to be restricted from doing business unlike national brand stores (which continued doing business), knowing the impact would be huge ... and it certainly was.

I will also offer my opinion on CERB cheques being handed out so liberally. Again, I believe today, as I did then, that if the government of the day had not forced small local businesses to shut down, spending those billions of dollars would have been unnecessary.

In the early stages of the pandemic, I said openly that the impact of COVID restrictions would be greater than the illness itself. My words were duly recorded in *The Winkler Morden Voice*, and after that, I was ridiculed by the medical staff, who said I didn't understand or support the "evidence" of science. Antagonizing the medical sector was not my intent. In my role as mayor, I decided to make a video with one of our long-term physicians, Dr. Klassen, encouraging people to listen to the doctors who delivered their babies, the ones they trusted to do their surgeries, the professionals who assisted them as they walked through the dark days of losing a loved one. After that, I was accused of picking sides on this issue, especially after I decided I would take the vaccine. Suddenly, in Winkler at least, the freedom demanded by some applied only to those who agreed with them, not to those who took the vaccine. Personally, I have never made any distinction between vaccinated or unvaccinated individuals. I still believe that it is each individual's right to decide, but that is where this should end.

Then there was the mask issue. Wow! Did that upset people! On one occasion, I entered the Super Store to pick up a jar of coffee, unaware of the policy of needing to wear a mask there.

No signs were visible, no one was enforcing it, so I ran in, asked a person where I could find the coffee and ran out. Not fifteen minutes! Next thing I knew, Facebook had dubbed me as the worst of community offenders! Disobedient to the law!

One visitor informed me that, because I took the vaccine, I would die in two years. In my office, I was told that Canada was no longer controlled by the Canadian government but had actually been taken over by some Central American "Queen" and we were now under her complete control. It was simply mind-boggling how the resentment rose and was spread by people vulnerable and naïve enough to believe it. We received letters from persons claiming they were descendants of and adhered to the Davidic Kingdom, and they were therefore exempt from any law. The situation was bizarre at best and difficult to ignore.

I believed differences of opinion should not tear communities or families or churches apart. In fact, this should never have become a church issue at all. This was a government issue, and the fight should have remained there as far as personal health choices were concerned. You don't like the decisions? Make sure you address the ones that made those rules, not your church and certainly not the business following the rules or the waitress that served you. Until the laws were changed, we were required to obey them.

I have compassion for those who spent a lifetime caring for others in the medical world, only to lose their jobs, not for any wrongdoing, but because political pressure made them choose between their profession and their conviction.

I also understand the truckers' dilemma and their desire to make a national statement. The fact they lost their jobs certainly contributed to current inflation, increased costs to consumers and product shortages. There are so many issues that are wrong, and these must be addressed with grace and respect, not with vengeance against businesses that are suffering or by protesting the businesses that were forced to comply. Simply being a presence in Ottawa asking for an audience was not too much to ask. Being met with arrogance and name-calling was unacceptable. However, staying till the public majority turned against the truckers was unfortunate, and spending multiple millions at the hearings only exacerbated the controversy in the public sphere. I actually asked the truckers, "Please, after you've received an audience with the opposition leader and the contender for the party leadership, hand over the reins to allow them to take the cause forward for you."

Then there was the education system. The need to self-educate online caused immeasurable damage to children's education and mental health. At the same time, there was an uprising because students were being asked to help protect themselves and others by wearing a simple mask. Masks were an inconvenience and protected us in the same way as sneezing into your elbow, but for some reason this mask became a cause to fight for our religious or health rights.

At one point, Winkler was even asked to close an outdoor skate park, further alienating our youth. In this regard, we were able to convince the inspectors that the ruling was inappropriate.

In the COVID years, 2020 to 2022, our Meridian Exhibition Centre changed operating procedures thirty-eight times to accommodate the amendments we needed to adhere to! Can you imagine the cost to our community and the outrage directed at the city, especially when the vaccinated had access to the facility and the unvaccinated did not? Again, the angered people threatened not to pay a portion of their taxes because we had created an apartheid situation right in our own community! Yes, these were the challenges we faced, but we stood strong, governing what we were responsible for and complying with the rules and restrictions forced on us, whether we agreed or not.

In the meantime, we continued to address the barrage of social media accusations. There was a lot of chatter on Facebook, and I received notice from the provincial justice department of threats on my life, but in their opinion, the risk to my safety was minimal. Every time another issue blew up, we consented to interviews with the mainstream media who were constantly sitting on our streets. Managing community was one thing, addressing false and misleading charges was quite another, and it did not help our situation. Irate posters on social media had no idea what we could or could not do. Still, they appeared determined to undermine the situation and drive people against one another based on one concern: for or against a vaccine, full stop. Individuals under the "umbrella" of loving their community were simply bound and determined to create the community they wanted (originating solely from their opinions) rather than being part of a city that was focused and united on the wonderful things that had already been accomplished by a council working hard for the entire community and providing the necessities for building a strong future after this crisis had passed. Plans to create a vibrant regional exhibition centre were not dependent on current crises or inconveniences; the centre was a need for the future.

As I look at the society we have today, it appears to be increasingly broken, and the rise in mental health issues is sad. Divorce rates have skyrocketed, the medical system is fractured and suicides are escalating because people have lost hope. Inflation has been going through the roof due to the policies and cover-ups of federal governments around the world. Printing money for circulation certainly has not solved any long-term concerns, but has in fact added more.

For the churches, COVID restrictions meant live-streaming services, opening up interaction with millions more than was ever possible within the walls of the church. This has brought new meaning to the command of Jesus to go into all the world to preach the gospel. Perhaps it will change the church from being or becoming a "social club" into an organism that cares for those who are in need and long for a Saviour. Certainly, today, there are people in distress at virtually every doorstep. What is our reaction? The world has become so transient, and the people who once were impossible to reach are on our own doorsteps today looking for hope. What is essentially the role of government and what are our responsibilities toward government? What did Jesus demonstrate?

"For even the Son of Man did not come to be served, but to serve, and to give his life as a ransom for many" Mark 10:45 (NIV).

As those who believe, that is our role. We are called to be His ambassadors, not "world fixers," which seems to have become our goal. Think about our future. Perhaps we need to adjust our focus on what really matters, take one step at a time, reach out to the ones we can reach and do our part to help society become a better place!

These were the questions that mattered to me: How do we survive as a community when there is so much controversy? How do we present ourselves as a caring, respected community while surrounded with in-fighting and division? Nationally and around the world, certainly the damage done was more severe than the initial impact of the disease, as devastating as that was. This will take generations to repair, if that is even possible. However, if we listen, the good that comes out of this will be the key to changing the future.

I believe and accept that any change I can make in my community has a direct impact on our future, but I am not here to

A Scrappy Little Nobody

change world events or fix global problems. I continue to trust in a God who has proven Himself to be trustworthy. Knowing that my future is held in His hands gives me peace. My own life is like a lighted candle, one breath away from darkness and the end of life as I know it. Without eternal values, all I have, all my accomplishments, my whole existence means nothing, as salt that has lost its savour, a lighted lamp that is hidden.

* * *

"You are the salt of the earth; but if the salt loses its flavor, how shall it be seasoned? It is then good for nothing but to be thrown out and trampled underfoot by men. You are the light of the world. A city that is set on a hill cannot be hidden. Nor do they light a lamp and put it under a basket, but on a lampstand, and it gives light to all who are in the house. Let your light so shine before men, that they may see your good works and glorify your Father in heaven" Matthew 5:13–16 (NKJV).

* * *

What follows are some major growth accomplishments in my sixteen years as Mayor of Winkler.

A "Balanced" Approach

Veteran's cenotaph move to the Bethel Park

A Scrappy Little Nobody

Bethel Heritage Park in downtown Winkler at the former Bethel Hospital site, where I received my surgery from Dr. C.W. Wiebe in 1949

Greg Ens Memorial Park, in memory of long-time friend and business leader Greg Ens, who passed away from cancer

Meridian Exhibition Centre

A "Balanced" Approach

Nine-storey seniors centre, assisted care and affordable senior's housing Buhler Active Living Centre downtown

A Scrappy Little Nobody

Icon Technologies RV replacement parts manufacturing

SteelTech manufacturing environmentally friendly biofuel stoves

Spenst Bros. Meats Pizza manufacturing 7,000 pizzas per day

THIRTY-ONE:
Reflections

Looking back over seventy years, from a traumatic birth to being bullied on school bus rides, a teenage marriage, the business world and beyond, I believe that God's angels have guided and protected me all along a way that now seems surreal, a mere blur. Over time, I learned to depend on God for my health, my finances and my future. I am convinced that He listens to my call and that's why I believe it is important to listen to others. Listening to God when doors open and trusting Him to walk me through them are the moments I cherish most.

Thinking back on all the stories of my life, I recognize the essential thread of communication. Effective communication is key to weathering every significant life passage or event. To be successful in any area of life, I have found it is essential to express myself well, clearly and with enthusiasm. Once I lose sight of this goal, trust disappears and relationships stagnate and break apart. Being married for the second time, I can say that the importance of communication is no different; it is always vital. In my first experience of dating, it was Eleanor's honesty and conviction that brought me to a new way of seeing myself and an awareness of the importance of my relationship with God. I came to know Him as my Saviour, my guide and the source of my strength because every breath is a gift. As my friend, He wants to hear from me through my prayers and that has become central to my life. I am thankful for the support I received from my family and from Eleanor, my wife of forty-six years.

I am grateful God gave me another opportunity to find joy in being married to Valerie, who gave me the courage to continue in my last term in office. From our first meeting, having that open conversation with her and with the many people we met that evening was critical to forming a trust and a new beginning for both of us. I recall the morning after meeting her, how vital it was for me to connect with all my kids to assure them how much they mattered to me and tell them about this new personal friend in my life. Just as my marriage with Eleanor would not have survived without keeping the lines open between us, neither would my marriage with Valerie be flourishing without communication.

* * *

I recall a former vice-president of Cargill telling a group of managers, "Some of you claim to have thirty years of experience, but I see some of you have had one experience thirty times!" It is not our years on the job that matters. It's what we learned during that time and have put to good use. Reflecting on the circumstances I faced before I decided to leave a full-time job with all the financial security I could ask for, giving it all up to start my own business, I remember an underlying feeling of not being heard, that I was being "used." Over time, I've learned there is value in listening to everyone, whether they agree with me or not. Whether they are "successful," struggle mentally or materially, or have social status has never made any difference to me. Every person is important.

Reflections

Now, as I consider my sixteen years in the mayor's chair, I recall that opportunities to listen and be heard were plentiful. Fellow councillors and I did not always agree, but we had learned to listen, hearing each other as equals and as valuable contributors to a common cause. I recall only one vote in council when, in my role as mayor, I used my voice to break a tie. Otherwise, though intense conversations took place as we prepared for the vote, we listened earnestly to each other and then brought the matter at hand to the council table. There was no need for political posturing.

The most controversial time would prove to be the pandemic, with all the restrictions and the opposition from community members with differing perspectives. We listened (making a case on Facebook was not necessarily communicating) and decided it would be wise to abide by the law and push for change. We resolved that it would be hazardous to risk public money to defend our position in court. As we see today, those court cases are costing millions, including money donated to churches that decided to ignore directives and thumbed their noses at authorities.

I believe the biggest mistake made by any political party is considering themselves "above" input from lower levels of government. Instead of listening to the people they serve, many politicians continue to choose to listen to individual experts who have never been in their community. Those politicians then decide on a recommendation from a totally uninformed perspective. I am reminded of the NDP government disregarding public input and municipal concerns about police boards, coming to consult with stakeholders after the decision had already been made. No timely communication. These same actions were repeated when obligatory municipal amalgamations were introduced with apparent consultation, but the process and criteria had already been set and were forced upon municipalities. Obviously, in both cases it caused enormous distrust and broken relationships. In similar fashion, the issue with the drought in 2021. We thought the government was coming to listen, but they couldn't wait to conclude the conversation, and with no team consultation, they simply cited what they had previously decided was the best solution.

I believe the same issues arise on a municipal level when people stop listening to ratepayers and depend entirely on the "expertise" of staff. I recall dealing with Winkler Aquifer when we needed to extract more water. Professionals who knew the aquifer held public information meetings to inform the public, answer any questions and address our concerns.

I fully understand the need for technical advice from professionals, but that is a challenging and more indirect way to convey information when dealing with matters that are obviously heavy on the hearts of ratepayers. People may not have been given all the information, and if they have opposing opinions, chances are they don't understand the full picture. Sometimes it's okay to simply disagree, and when we do, we need to learn to move on and not park there stewing in our differences.

As a young boy, I did not appreciate being bullied. Until I learned to truly forgive those who wronged me, I found ways to hide and internalize the hurt. As a politician, on occasion, the tactics used by elected officials felt very similar. The process of telling my story here reopened the old wounds, and I discovered that I am still learning that vital lesson of forgiving and moving on. It is difficult but essential, and I am committed to continue seeking reconciliation, even now.

*　*　*

Reflections

As I reflect on the quality of life we enjoy in Winkler today, I see a tremendous difference from what I saw sixteen years earlier. It truly has become a place where people come to dream, build and live. Thank you to all the hard-working staff that keeps our city attractive and functioning well, along with the hundreds of volunteers spending thousands of hours creating and maintaining city beautification. I am proud to have been able to serve such an awesome community as mayor for sixteen years. I continue to look forward to new opportunities ahead.

My leadership style has always been to look out for the average person rather than to look for the elite or refined individual. Impacting people and things that typically receive little or no attention but are still valuable and worthy of care has been and is a part of who I am. Through listening to people and understanding their perspective and their needs, I have learned to stand up for others, persuade some and respect those I disagree with. I have been able to face the daunting challenges of my life with boldness and unreserved commitment. Against all odds, God saved my life as an infant and then later equipped me to serve, gifting me with the resources I needed for family, business and community though He still allowed me to experience pain. And in each situation, He stilled my fears and brought me into a closer walk with Him. I see God at work through His protection, His wisdom, and His forgiveness all along the way, daily increasing my ability to trust Him.

* * *

I am grateful for God's plans for me and for Dr. Wiebe's timely intervention following my traumatic early life and death challenge in Winkler's Bethel Hospital days after my birth. My life came full circle and I returned to Winkler to live, work and serve. Against all odds, God spared my life in multiple near-death episodes, gave spiritual light and drew me to Himself in relationship, guiding this high school dropout through challenging pathways in family life, the corporate world, entrepreneurial business and the political world.

These are the memories that remain in my heart. Today, I thank God for the opportunity to give back. My life is richer for having listened, learned and served the ones who allowed me to lead.

Printed in Canada